HEARTSTRINGS

JILL BRISCOE

Tyndale House Publishers, Inc.
Wheaton, Illinois

Library of Congress Cataloging-in-Publication Data

Briscoe, Jill.
   Heartstrings / Jill Briscoe.
     p. cm.
   ISBN 0-8423-1461-X (sc : alk. paper)
   1. Contentment—Religious aspects—Christianity.   2. Satisfaction—Religious aspects—Christianity.   3. Joy—Religious aspects—Christianity.   I. Title.
BV4647.C7B75   1997
248.4—dc21   97-33490

Printed in the United States of America

04 03 02 01 00 99 98 97
10 9 8 7 6 5 4 3 2 1

TABLE OF CONTENTS

INTRODUCTION

Have you lost your joy? Do you feel that it's been a long time since the Lord touched the heartstrings of your innermost being?

The people of Israel felt like that. They were in captivity in Babylon. God's people were refugees by coercion, slaves of cruel masters. They were far away from home with only bad memories for company.

The Babylonians were a rough bunch to deal with, just as they are today. They represent our lost world, the third of our world, we are told, who have never heard of such a thing as a relationship with a holy God through Christ's redemptive work on their behalf. People who live, as the hymn says

> As if no Christ has shed His precious blood,
> As if they owed no homage to their God.

The Babylonians in the Israelites' lives were not only rough but cynical. "Go on, sing us one of the songs of Zion," they taunted the Israelites. They weren't a bit surprised when the Israelites replied bitterly, "How can we sing the songs of the Lord—in a foreign land?" Their harps, once sounding songs of Zion, hung silently on the trees beside the river, where the captives were camped.

Of course the Babylonians knew that people don't feel like singing when they've seen their parents murdered, houses pillaged, and infants' brains bashed out on the cobblestones. Who is going to rise to an occasion like that and sing a song?

But then they heard it. *A harp.* An old man with fire in his eyes was singing! He was singing one of the songs of Zion! It was a beautiful song—a song of comfort and of hope. A song about a Shepherd gently leading those with young. A song about eternity and a God who inhabited it, owned it, and was offering to share it with those who would put their faith in him.

Who was this old man? He was one of Israel's temple musicians; they, like the other refugees, were far away from home, too. They were sitting by the waters of Babylon along with the rest of the captives. But they were different from the others in an important way.

If we could go back to that time and look carefully, we would see that every tree in sight was festooned with harps *except* the ones under which these music makers were resting after a hard day's slave labor. There they were, harps in hand, singing songs! They sang a message from the writings of the prophet Isaiah to God's discouraged people.

The songs started with the words:

> *Comfort, comfort my people,*
> *says your God. . . .*
> *Those who hope in the Lord*
> *will renew their strength.*
> *They will soar on wings like eagles;*
> *they will run and not grow weary,*
> *they will walk and not be faint.*
> (Isa. 40:1, 31)

The Babylonians must have thought they'd never heard such a beautiful song in all of their lives. It made them yearn for something—they didn't know quite what—something these holy men among the captives of Israel had that they didn't have and that the rest of the Israelite slaves didn't appear to be enjoying.

Now *we* know what that was, don't we! We know that Israel had lost touch with the source of life and joy—God himself. Yet Pastor Isaiah, who had written this song years ago, had come close enough to God to be forgiven and had stayed close enough to be strengthened. The writer of the words the temple musicians now sang had learned to *wait*. The song was about waiting on the Lord for all one needs—to have joy in life and to be a blessing to the hurting world, believers and nonbelievers alike. Now Isaiah's words, written in the past, were bringing blessing to a painful present for the captives by the waters of sorrow.

The Babylonians Are Listening

Today the Babylonians are listening to us just as surely as they were to the temple musicians. They are watching those of us who profess to be God lovers. They see our husbands and wives die, our children rebel. They watch us get sick just as they get sick. They observe us as we lose our jobs, are displaced, are on welfare, or are mistreated. And the way we respond to suffering preaches a more powerful sermon than any religious, silver-tongued rhetoric could.

The Israelites had an incredible opportunity to use the pressure of their circumstances to wait on the Lord. Their lives could have been a living pulpit out of which God could preach and teach and reach his lost world. But look at them and listen to them! Look at their body language, their exhausted faces, the bitter twisted mouths. Their devotion has dried up—they are speechless, songless, loveless, hopeless. They are harpless, hapless, hopeless harpists.

They need comfort and encouragement first. Then they need

to be challenged before they can be used to bless and help Babylonians. And the men with the fire in their eyes know it. They say, "Have we got a message for you: *Wait on the Lord.*" That's the answer; that's the secret. There's joy in that, joy to be found, *strength* to be found—in God's waiting room.

God is the builder and maker of such an internal palace. There is a place within us where he's waiting for us to wait—to wait, hope, look, and cast our burdens on him. This internal waiting room is a place to exchange our weakness for his power. To let him play the heartstrings of our life.

Are you in God's waiting room? What are you waiting for? A marriage to be mended, a child to give just a little indication that he or she *likes* belonging to you? A job, a home of your own, reconciliation? A baby to be conceived or born? Or are you perhaps just waiting in "nothing much is happening land" for the joy and vitality of your spiritual life to be renewed?

Well, God is waiting—for you to wait.

When we learn how to do that, the wind of the Spirit will lift us up above our dreadful days, as well as our mundane days, and we will start to cope—with hope! Yes, we shall!

Imagine yourself to be one of those men or women, teenagers or children sitting under your particular weeping willow tree, having hung up your harp—your joy. Which tree have you chosen?

The Trees Where Harps Are Hung

Perhaps you have lost your joy at the grief tree. Maybe you have lost people you loved. Not only did you stop singing the day your beloved died or divorced you—it seemed the birds stopped singing, too.

If not the grief tree, maybe your harp is hung on the gripe tree, the grudge tree, the growth tree, or the grind tree. Then there are the grating, gloom, girl, gift, and geriatric trees. All these trees represent circumstances, situations, and states of well- (or not so well!) being that cause us to hang up our joy. These trees have been around for a long time.

As you read these pages, it is my prayer that you will find a new song to sing—a song to your God, to his people, and to your world. As you wait on the Lord, you will find Jehovah to be the God of eternity, who created the ends of the earth. This God isn't finished—with you or with your life.

> *This God—*
> *doesn't wear out or decay.*
> *The everlasting God—lasts.*
> *The powerful one is never powerless!*
> *The changeless one—doesn't.*
> *The unwearied one is not wearied by weariness.*
> *He faints not, is not fatigued.*
> *The tireless One—doesn't tire,*
> *and those who wait upon the Lord*
> *shall renew—gain new—strength,*
> *exchange his strength for their weakness.*
> *He, God, self-imparts his energy, his strength;*
> *he gives power to the tired and worn-out.*
> *He is the source of all joy.*
> *—J. B.*

CHAPTER ONE

THE GRIEF TREE

By the rivers of Babylon, there we sat down, yea,
we wept, when we remembered Zion.

Psalm 137:1, KJV

I was standing in Croatia just across the border from Bosnia, talking with a refugee family who had just fled to safety. They were gazing across the road to a hill where their house stood—a house they had just abandoned as the enemy rolled into their village. The lights from the little house glinted in the dusk. Only forty-eight hours ago this family had been living as they wanted, where they wanted, and how they wanted. Now strangers sat around their kitchen table sifting through their private papers and playing with their photographs. Soon these hostile strangers would sleep in this family's beds.

I looked at my watch; it was time to enter the church where we were processing the new refugees. It was evening, and a short worship service being offered. I invited this family to attend, and they followed me inside as the organ began to play. Sitting in the old church pews, dumbstruck with shock and grief, the refugees asked me silently with their blank faces, "How do you expect us to sing the songs of Zion in this foreign land?"

How indeed? Yet at least this particular family was intact! As I looked around me I realized others were not! It's one thing to lose everything you own; it's altogether another thing to lose every*one* you own. It's at times like these you realize how much more important people are than things.

> ***It's at times like these you realize how much more important people are than things.***

It's hard to sing a song of any sort when you are experiencing grief, isn't it? Whether you live in Bosnia, Hong Kong, Frankfurt, Rwanda, Europe, or the United States, grief takes the song right out of life. "I was expecting to be a grandmother," a gentle, silver-haired Canadian told me. "Then my daughter had an abortion. I feel I've had one, too—I've lost my joy!" An elder in a church in Holland confided in me that his daughter had fallen in love with a girl! "She left home and moved in with her last month," he said with tears in his eyes. "I have cried until I can cry no more." He, too, had hung up his happiness. Loss can visit our life in all sorts of ways on all sorts of days, bringing an excruciating emotional pain that takes our breath away and that nothing seems to touch.

The people of God in Old Testament times knew all about this. Like the refugees in Bosnia, they had suffered the loss of all things and were no longer free to live how they wanted, where they wanted, and when they wanted (a freedom, I might add, most of us tend to take for granted). The Babylonians had arrived in Jerusalem and dragged most of the population off to Babylon. There they placed them in work camps and subjected them to slave labor.

The Israelites had experienced the deepest grief. Fathers and mothers and grandparents too aged to make the forced march from Jerusalem to Babylon had been dispatched without mercy by the invading forces. Likewise, the infants and babies were smashed against the rocks. Small battered bodies littered the bloodred streets of the Holy City. After witnessing such atrocities, it was hard for the Israelites to close their eyes at night and shut out those awful images. How would you ever get over seeing those you love so brutally murdered?

If grief touches us, that's one thing—but if it touches our children, that's quite another! Henry Gariepy addresses this pain in his excellent book on Job (*Portraits of Perseverance,* [Wheaton, Ill.: Victor Books, 1991], 45): "We will not only have our own problems; the problems of those we love and care for and for whom we have such high hopes and dreams, hit us with full force as well. When tragedy strikes them, the quakes in their lives are registered on the Richter scale of our own hearts." Which of us with children cannot empathize? Many of us can fully understand the response of the people of God when their tormentors demanded they sing "Praise the Lord and Hallelujah!"

Is God There, Is He Fair, Does He Care?

Today many of us find ourselves in foreign environments and unexpected places or situations. For instance, some grandparents would never have thought they would stand in a divorce court watching their grandchildren divided up between parents. How could a mother I spoke to not long ago cope with the news that her beautiful Christian daughter, returning fresh from the mission field, had been infected with the AIDS virus through an accident with a dirty needle? When our world falls apart, we may well find ourselves losing our confidence in God, in other people, in ourselves, and in very life itself.

The Lord's people in the Old Testament lost their freedom, friends, and family; some lost everything and everyone. They suffered dreadfully. Their hope and confidence in the God who had been faithful to their fathers were severely tested. In the past they had been Jehovah's precious possession, his called-out people—the apple of his eye! He had rolled back the seas and the rivers in front of them so they could escape their enemies on dry land. He had caused their Jerichos to collapse and led them triumphantly out of slavery into the Promised Land. But now their temple lay in ruins, their leaders were murdered, their precious scrolls were burned, their history was derided, and their Holy City was ransacked. It looked as though God had forsaken and forgotten them. The despair of that loss seemed to outweigh all others.

In times past they had cried, "If God be for us, who can be against us?" Now, cowering under the whips of their masters, they wondered miserably, *If God be against us, then who can be for us?* Such misery knows little music. Instead of singing, they asked each other despairingly, "Is God there, is he fair, does he care?" As they bent their backs in the boiling sun, they wondered aloud, "Has he left us to the consequences of our own stupidity?" "God must have abandoned us forever," some said. "We rejected him and now all the evidence suggests that he has rejected us!" By the waters of Babylon there were many weeping willows festooned with harps.

But one tree was empty. Underneath it, in the cool of the evening, an aged man with fire in his eyes was singing a song. He was singing it to the people of God, but the Babylonians who stood guard over their captives couldn't help but hear it, too. It was a song of comfort, a song of Zion, a song of joy. And it went like this:

> "Comfort, yes, comfort my people," says your God. "Speak tenderly to Jerusalem, and tell her that her sad days are gone. Her sins are pardoned, and I have punished her in full for all her sins." (Isa. 40:1-2, TLB)

Who was this old man? He was a part of the nation of Israel. He was either a priest or a temple musician. He was a Jewish exile. He had been carried away to Babylon along with everyone else. He had lost his freedom and his precious sacred scrolls. He was far, far away from his beloved city and sweet holy temple. No doubt people he loved had been tortured and slaughtered before his eyes. Possibly he had lost everything and everyone. So how on earth was he managing to sing such a song in this unexpected place? And what a song it was! It was a song of divine encouragement and promise, a song of overwhelming confidence in the Shepherd of Israel, who would surely find his wandering sheep and return them to his fold.

Comfort is a contagious thing!

This man was getting his encouragement from the writings of Isaiah, and in the midst of his troubles he experienced the joy of the Lord. Indeed, the "joy of the Lord was his strength," for he'd found a sanctuary within his heart where he and his God walked and talked in the garden of his soul in the cool of the day. He'd found an "internal waiting room," and there waiting for him was the God of all comfort.

Comfort is a contagious thing! God's comfort first comforts us, and then it spills out of our life to comfort others. This is what the apostle Paul confirms in the New Testament.

 What a wonderful God we have—he is the Father of our Lord Jesus Christ, the source of every mercy, and the one who so wonderfully comforts and strengthens us in our hardships and trials. And why does he do this? So that when others are troubled, needing our sympathy and encouragement, we can pass on to them this same help and comfort God has given us. You can be sure that the more we undergo sufferings for Christ, the more he will shower us with his comfort and encouragement. (2 Cor. 1:3-5, TLB)

Paul sees this trouble as a springboard for action—a chance to help others as he had been helped.

> We are in deep trouble for bringing you God's comfort and salvation. But in our trouble God had comforted us—and this, too, to help you: to show you from our personal experience how God will tenderly comfort you when you undergo these same sufferings. He will give you the strength to endure. (2 Cor. 1:6-7, TLB)

Singing the Comfort Song

Paul knew what it was to suffer the "loss of all things." Several hundred years after the Babylonian captivity, a new church in Corinth was encountering grave difficulties. Christians were being persecuted, hunted down like animals, and killed. Some of the men, women, and children would have been Paul's own converts. Yet Paul knew they were with Christ, which was "far better."

Sitting by my dying mother's bedside, I realized she would soon be released into life—real life, eternal life. As I sat there, I picked up my New Testament and went to my internal "waiting room." As I listened to my mother's labored breathing, I reread in John's Gospel the story of Jesus standing outside the tomb of Lazarus. He shouted,

> "Lazarus, come out!" And Lazarus came—bound up in the gravecloth, his face muffled in a head swath. Jesus told [those watching], "Unwrap him and let him go!" (John 11:43-44, TLB)

As I read these words, I looked up. My mother's face was still. I was suddenly searingly aware that her labored breathing had stopped. I looked down at my Bible, huge tears of grief splashing onto its pages. Through my tears I read again that great shout of the Lord's:

"Lazarus, come out!"—and then I saw in my mind's eye what had just happened. I saw the other side of death, right then, even as I still sat on this side, in my terrifying "now." My mother had "come out" as Jesus had called her name, and in my mind's eye I saw that one who'd given me birth, who had been bound hand and foot with the graveclothes of cancer. Jesus was telling those who stood around her tomb—the angels themselves—to "unwrap her and let her go"!

"And she that was dead came forth," I murmured, my eye following the story in John 11. A great flood of joy began to immerse me in its warm waves of praise. The nurse came into the room. "She's home. No more night, no more pain, no more tears, no more dying!" I said simply. The nurse cried. And so I sang her my song born out of my grief and overwhelming loss. A song of comfort and of joy. The words of my song were: "Absent from the body, present with the Lord."

The tomb can be a place of both fear and comfort for the believer. There is the fear of losing the familiar and loved one, and yet the joy of knowing that for those who have gone to be with the Lord, there is an incredible environment waiting for them where Jesus himself is and where loved ones who have preceded us wait for us.

The problem is that what is best for them is worst for us! We cannot but mourn their passing. Like Martha and Mary weeping at Lazarus's tomb, we believe the only thing that could ever bring some vestige of peace and comfort to our riven life would be to have our beloved "Lazarus" returned to our arms again.

But think of it from Lazarus's perspective. The story is told in John's Gospel. Lazarus gets sick and dies. Probably in that day and age his was a premature and painful death. It appears the illness was sudden. Within a week of the sisters' alerting Jesus to Lazarus's illness, their brother was dead. Actually, he was dead to Martha and Mary, yet more alive than he had ever been! He was in a place where flowers never fade, no one ever gets sick again, and things beyond his wildest dreams or imaginings were happening. The Bible says, "No eye has seen, no ear has heard, no mind has conceived what God has prepared for those who love him" (1 Cor. 2:9). Lazarus was surely thinking, *It's heaven to be in heaven!*

Then Jesus came to his tomb and shouted, "Lazarus, come out!" Can't you hear Lazarus groan, "Oh no!" I'm sure he said, "Not again. You mean go back to suffer and die a second time? Must I leave 'here' to go 'there'?" Yet he had to respond to the voice of resurrection and life standing outside his earthly tomb—so he obeyed.

But who benefited? Lazarus or Martha and Mary? Sometimes we have a very poor view of heaven, don't you think?

When we seem to be surrounded by the horror and loneliness of death, our comfort is to know that those we love so very much are seeing our Lord's face. Though they are out of our arms, they are into his. The Christian has this song to sing! When my father died, a friend sent me a poem that helped me remember how much better it was for him to be with God in heaven than with us on earth. I revisited the poem at my mother's deathbed and found comfort in it:

> *Better to be like a lark on high,*
> *singing for joy 'neath a cloudless sky.*
> *Better to know no sorrow or pain,*
> *no dying or death, but to live again.*
> *Better far better with Christ to be,*
> *living and loved through eternity.*
> —Anonymous

On my knees, I knew that what was worst for me was best for her, and I took down my harp from the grief tree and got ready to sing a song.

I sang my song many times in the days following my mother's death. I sang it to the people of God, and I sang it to the Babylonians. And many listened to me because even Babylonians have loved ones who get sick and die. Even Babylonians have to sit beside their parents waiting for their breathing to stop. They need to know there's a waiting room where God is to be found. There is a sanctuary inside a forgiven sinner, where comfort is given, hope is birthed, and joy—incredible joy—is waiting for us. Others need to know that God is waiting for us to wait!

Absent from the Body, Present with the Lord

One night I was busy putting our two oldest grandchildren to bed. Dan, nine, and Mike, eight, stripped off their clothes, leaving them in two little heaps on the floor. Bath time was fun—and wet as usual—and soon pajamas were on, and the two small boys were tucked into bed. Bible verses were read and prayers said, and my hand was on the light switch before Dan said, "Nana, I was watching TV tonight. There was a funeral, and the box [casket] was in the church. Nana," he said with a note of fear in his young voice, "how long will I be in the box?"

"How long will I be in the box?"

I came back from the door and sat on his bed. Reaching for his Bible and turning to the verse, I said, "Not one second, Dan. See it says here: 'Absent from the body, present with the Lord.' " He looked relieved, though puzzled. "Then, Nana," he said, "what goes in the box?" I looked down at the floor. There lay the two small piles of clothes, undisturbed, where the kids had left them before their baths. "Look, Dan and Mike," I said, pointing to the clothes. "These clothes are like our bodies. The real person—the real Dan or the real Mike—lives inside the clothes. When your body dies, it's like the clothes—the body—dropping off. That's what goes in the box!"

There was silence as they absorbed this piece of new information. Their eyes were fastened on the clothes. "Will we be naked then, Nana?" asked Mike, ever the practical one.

"No, Mike." I laughed. "God will give us glory clothes that will make our old clothes look like rags."

"Does everyone know about this?" inquired Mike, awed.

"No, Mike," I answered, "that's why Papa Stu and Nana and all the family are busy telling everyone."

"Joey doesn't know," Mike said. (Joey was a cute little Babylonian boy—one of Mike's good friends at school.) "I'll tell him tomorrow."

"What will you tell him, Mike?"

"I'll tell him he doesn't have to be in the box," he said simply. The next day Mike told Joey. He sang him a song about the Lord and his salvation and that we don't have to worry about dying if we know Jesus. *Lord, I pray Joey is the first of many to hear the songs of Zion our sweet grandchildren will sing, in whatever foreign land they find themselves in the future.*

Are You under the Grief Tree?

One day a friend of mine woke up completely depressed and tearful for no reason she could think of. It wasn't until she was at work, typing a letter, that she typed in the date and realized it was the one-year anniversary of her father's death. So she called her mother and grandmother, and they cried together. It was grief, not depression. And they needed to remember that beloved parent and cry and say again that they were glad he wasn't suffering anymore.

Many times people are fatigued, sad, or frightened because they haven't faced their grief and learned to enter that waiting room. Sometimes, like my friend, we don't realize that what we are experiencing is grief. At other times we don't seem to be able to stop grieving even though we are fully aware that is what we are doing!

After my mother died, I found myself crying at the drop of a hat. Anything that reminded me of her would set me off. She used to put everything in plastic bags and secure them with rubber bands. The sight of a plastic bag or rubber band was enough to trigger a flood of tears. Sometimes I would be in church and catch sight of an elderly lady with a similar silhouette or hairstyle or even the same smile, and I'd catch my breath and have to get out of the sanctuary to get hold of myself.

The thing that helped me in the end was realizing the hope I had—the eternal hope and confidence in my mother's salvation. I began to praise God for that every time such an incident would happen. My dear mother had put her faith in Jesus shortly before she died, and I had never had the joy of sharing fellowship with her. Shortly after, I began practicing a song of Zion instead of a dirge every time something would trigger my grief. I awoke one morning with perfect peace of mind and heart. As I entered the waiting room (where God was waiting for me to wait), I had a new thought: *Now she understands. Now she knows what happened to me when I was converted to Christ all those years ago—now she really understands!* Then the tears stopped.

My grief was evidenced by my tears. You may have tears or other clues in your life that you're under the grief tree. We don't have to experience the death of a loved one to grieve. Loss takes its toll when we move to a new place and away from the familiar one, when we lose a job or a friend. And grief comes to us when we say good-bye to a dream that hasn't worked out the way we'd planned.

If you are filled with sadness, go into your waiting room and wait for the Lord to show you what loss you are grieving. Once you face your grief, you can begin to be comforted.

How to Sing When You're under the Grief Tree

How can we learn to wait on the Lord to renew our joy and strength when we suffer grief and loss? How do we learn songs arising from our pain that we need to sing and that the Babylonians need to hear?

Make time and space to wait on the Lord.

The word *wait* in this passage in Isaiah 40 means to hope—to have overwhelming confidence in something! This "hope" chamber within us is a place where we learn the promises of a faithful God, who keeps his word no matter how far away we are from him. He himself inhabits this place. Look around the internal waiting room, and you'll find you've got company! God is, and God is here; he's not going anywhere. "I am with you always," he promised, "to the very end of the age" (Matt. 28:20). It doesn't matter where you live or what has happened to you, whether you have lost everything or everyone. There in a quiet internal place within the believer where he waits for you, you can dare to begin to believe in a better day. No matter how horrible it is by our particular waters of sorrow, there is a new day coming. "Weeping may go on all night, but in the morning there is joy" (Ps. 30:5, TLB). The most incredible and inspiring songs of the faith ever penned have been composed by these bitter waters of sorrow.

Only as we wait on God will we find the wings of the Spirit lifting us above our circumstances.

Horatio G. Spafford had established an extremely successful legal practice in Chicago. A Presbyterian layman with a keen interest in spiritual things, he enjoyed close relationships with D. L. Moody and other evangelical leaders of the day. He invested heavily in real estate along the shores of Lake Michigan, but then came a string of disasters he could never have foreseen. Horatio Spafford suddenly found himself by his own bitter waters of Babylon.

First his son died. Then the Chicago fire of 1871 wiped out his holdings. D. L. Moody and Ira Sankey were planning to campaign in Britain, and Horatio thought it would help his family to get a break if he and his wife and four daughters went with the evangelists. At the last minute he was delayed by business and sent his family on ahead of him on the SS *Ville du Havre*, intending to follow them as soon as he could get away. On November 22 there was an accident at sea, and the SS *Ville du Havre* sank within twelve minutes. Days later when the survivors were brought ashore in Cardiff, Wales, Mrs. Spafford cabled her husband: "Saved alone." Horatio left at once to join her. While at sea, near where it was believed his four girls had drowned, a song was born, a song birthed in deep, deep sorrows—the loss of a man's children, first a son and then four beloved daughters. A loss that surely resonated on the Richter scale of Horatio Spafford's heart. Comforted by his God at the depth of his grief, he refused to hang up his harp on a weeping willow tree but rather insisted on waiting on the Lord to renew his spiritual strength. These are the words he wrote:

> When peace, like a river, attendeth my way,
> When sorrows like sea billows roll;
> Whatever my lot, Thou hast taught me to say,
> "It is well, it is well with my soul."
>
> Tho' Satan should buffet, tho' trials should come,
> Let this blest assurance control,
> That Christ has regarded my helpless estate,
> And hath shed His own blood for my soul.
>
> My sin—O the bliss of this glorious thought,
> My sin—not in part, but the whole,
> Is nailed to the cross and I bear it no more,
> Praise the Lord, praise the Lord, O my soul!
>
> And, Lord, haste the day when the faith shall be sight,
> The clouds be rolled back as a scroll,

> *The trump shall resound and the Lord shall descend,*
> *"Even so"—it is well with my soul.*
> "It Is Well with My Soul," Horatio G. Spafford (1873)

If it is well with our souls, we will find that our God will never let the sea billows of any storm life throws at us submerge us in despair. Because he, the Man of Sorrows, bore our sin and grief on the cross, there is life and hope even in the middle of the worst tragedy. Only as we wait on God will we find the wings of the Spirit lifting us above our circumstances.

The thing that amazes me, however, about us failing, fallible, faithless folk who profess to belong to Jesus is the way we will do anything but resort to God's comfort. We will not wait in a quiet place for joyful faith and confidence to become the very breath that we breathe. Instead, we wait on circumstances, chance, someone's advice, books, tapes, radio, a friend, or our pastor. All of these may well help a little, but in the end it is Jehovah who is the God of eternity, who created the ends of the earth, who alone can lift our flagging spirit. This is the God who isn't finished—who doesn't wear out or decay. He is the everlasting one who lasts, the powerful one who is never powerless. He is the changeless one who doesn't change, the unwearied one who is not wearied by weariness. He fails not—is not fatigued. He is the tireless one who doesn't tire, and those who get around to running into his arms will find their strength renewed.

Don't waste the pain.

At the moment of writing I am sitting by my own bitter waters of Babylon. I find myself in a foreign land. Never in a thousand years did I expect to be in such a place as this. But I am asking the Lord that God would accomplish his mysterious and secret purposes in and through my life because of this personal crisis. A week or so ago as I was sitting on a plane feeling despondent, he began to give me a song to sing. It was not a song in a major key—but rather a minor one. But who says such music isn't beautiful and makes its own mark?

A friend who knew about my hurting heart had called to comfort me. In the course of our conversation she had said, "Don't waste the pain, Jill." The phrase caught my attention. So, capturing the moment, I sensed that he who waited with me gave me words:

> *Don't waste the pain*
> *let it prove thee.*
> *Don't stop the tears*
> *let them cleanse thee.*
> *Rest, cease the striving,*
> *soon you'll be arriving in His arms.*
> *Don't waste the pain*
> *let it drive thee*
> *deeper into God.*
> *He's waiting—and*
> *you should have come sooner!*
> —J. B.

Perhaps my song may comfort you who read the pages of this book. Stop waiting on everything and everyone else, and "let the pain drive thee—deeper into God!" If you do, I know you'll hear him say, "You should have come sooner!"

Don't try to figure out why.

One thing we should avoid as best we can is wasting too much energy trying to figure out the *whys*. "But that's impossible," I hear you say. "I have so many questions." Perhaps you could ask God a different question. How about asking *how* instead of *why*?

When Mary was visited by Gabriel and told she was to have a baby—and not just a baby but *the baby*, the one every Jewish girl hoped she would be privileged to bear—she didn't ask *why* but rather *how*. She could quite understandably have asked, "Why? And why now? Why here?" Instead, she simply asked, "How?" The answer to "How can I possibly do the will of God in this incredible situation?" was quite simple, given by the angel visitor: "The Holy Spirit . . ." Immediately Mary responded with a glad "I am the Lord's servant."

I have tried to train my reactions to behave in such an exemplary fashion. When my husband was needed to travel around the world as a leader and evangelist, I was tempted to ask, "Why? Why now? [We had small children and widowed mothers to care for.] Why here, far away from family to help me—why?" It was a struggle, but I managed to start asking, "How? How will I find the strength to live above these difficult circumstances, Lord? How will I be able to be a mother and a father to three small children?" When a "Why couldn't other men on the team take their turn on the road; why does it have to be my husband?" sort of question would raise its head, I'd counter it with, "Why *shouldn't* it be my husband? Thank you, Lord, for the privilege of being married to someone you are using so greatly! How can I be a partner at this time? How can I be both a mom and dad so he can go in peace, knowing things are taken care of at home base?" God's answers to my *how* questions were always the same. They were the answers Mary received from Gabriel. The Holy Spirit would overshadow me, and in his power the challenge would be faced and his will would be done.

So next time a *why* starts demanding to be heard, try running instantly to the waiting room in order for the *how* to begin. It is in our internal "still point"—our waiting room—that, as we worship, we will be helped to lay down our *whys* at his feet.

May such songs of submission and spiritual strength be songs even the heathen around us will take note of. May they engender a great longing for wholeness and saintliness in the hearts of those who listen.

LEARNING TO SING AGAIN

SPENDING TIME TOGETHER

For couples, families, Bible study groups, Sunday school classes, or for family devotions

1. Read Psalm 137 through. After reading the chapter, discuss which phrase, story, or Scripture struck home and why.

- What picture do you get of the Babylonians in the psalm?

- What picture do you get of the Israelites?

- Have you hung up your "harp" on the grief tree? If appropriate and without using names, share with the group your particular sorrow.

2. Read Isaiah 40 through. Which verses do you think would particularly encourage parents who have lost children?

3. Read the hymn on pages 15–16. In what does the hymn writer find his comfort? Where can we?

4. Spend some moments in prayer, asking God to give you strength and grace to bear private grief publicly. Pray you will not "waste the pain" God has allowed but let it drive you deeper into God.

5. Pray for each other.

6. Pray for people you know who have hung up their harps on the grief tree.

SPENDING TIME ALONE

1. Read one of the following books on grieving:

- *Life after Grief*, Lawrenz & Greene (Baker)

- *Good Grief*, Westberg (Fortress)

- *Grief for a Season*, Tengbom (Bethany House)

2. Spend time reading and thinking about the following passages of Scripture:

- Isaiah 40

- Psalm 23 and Isaiah 40:11

- James 1:2-5

- 2 Corinthians 1:3-7

3. Don't be afraid to cry or be angry. Do it in the waiting room with him. He understands; he's waiting for you to wait and to weep.

4. Talk to another Christian who has lost someone he or she loves and who has worked through the grief process.

5. Find a trusted friend to pray with and for you—such friends are to be found in the fellowship of his church.

6. Make a daily list of blessings that come out of grief, and thank God for them.

7. Volunteer to serve in a ministry with people who are worse off than yourself.

8. Start practicing asking *how* instead of *why*.

CHAPTER TWO

THE GRIPE TREE

*As far as I am concerned, God turned into good
what you meant for evil.*
Genesis 50:20, NLT

All of us know what it is to have a pity party. It is self-pity
that whines and whimpers whenever our heart is discontent. We feel sorry for ourselves for all sorts of reasons.
Perhaps we feel we're not tall enough, pretty enough, or athletic
enough. Some children can become obsessed simply because they
have brown eyes and they want blue eyes! Such was the case with
Amy Carmichael.

> *Just a tiny little child*
> *Three years old,*
> *And a mother with a heart*
> *All of gold.*
> *Often did that mother say,*
> *"Jesus hears us when we pray,*
> *For He's never far away*
> *And He always answers."*
>
> *Now that tiny little child*
> *Had brown eyes.*
> *And she wanted blue instead*
> *Like blue skies.*

For her mother's eyes were blue
Like forget-me-nots. She knew
All her mother said was true,
Jesus always answered.

So she prayed for two blue eyes,
Said, "Good night,"
Went to sleep in deep content
And delight.
Woke up early, climbed a chair
By a mirror. Where, O where
Could the blue eyes be? Not there;
Jesus hadn't answered.

Hadn't answered her at all;
Never more
Could she pray; her eyes were brown
As before.
Did a little soft wind blow?
Came a whisper soft and low,
"Jesus answered. He said, No:
Isn't No an answer?"

At a very early age, Amy Carmichael prayed for blue eyes, but her brown eyes stayed brown! A good thing, too, because Amy became a daring missionary in India, where blue eyes would have marked her as a foreigner. Sometimes we need to have faith to believe that no is an answer to prayer! No is an answer sometimes and for God's good reasons, not only in the matter of physical things, but in social and spiritual matters as well.

When Believers Give In to Self-Pity

God had said no to certain things his people wanted. They were told not to worship other gods. They had more or less complied, but their temple worship had become empty and meaningless—a mere ritual. God had told them their worship must not be like this; but they ignored him, and apostasy followed, which resulted in their beautiful temple being in ruins (Isa. 1:10-18).

The people of God felt very bad about it; however, they were not sorry for God but for themselves. They wept when they thought of Jerusalem and their temple rituals. They did not weep for their rebellious, contrary hearts. Now that there was no temple in which to worship, they did not realize their error and begin to worship God in spirit and in truth; they simply grumbled and mumbled as had been their habit since Moses led them out of Egypt. When you indulge in self-pity, it's a miserable affair. No joy in that! The people of God had truly hung up their harps on the gripe tree!

I've discovered that when I complain, my spirit is overwhelmed. A spirit of complaint leads to depression and spoils my relationships. I've observed that I can be sitting in a worship service and start to gripe inwardly about the music, the teenager's earrings in front of me, or the lighting or flowers on the platform! Immediately my spirit of worship disappears, and I am overwhelmed with a sense of discontent. The children of Israel were into complaining—especially in church. It did nothing to lift their spirits or fortify their souls.

So how do we stop ourselves from griping and grumbling, thereby losing our joy?

Christians, who should be the most thankful people in the world, often sound the most disgruntled. It's as if we feel the world owes us something instead of remembering it's we who owe the world! The apostle Paul thought of himself as in debt to humankind. He believed he owed them an explanation of the gospel. He also felt he owed them a life of service and sacrifice. He was, after all, rich beyond measure! He had come to know Christ, the priceless Son of God. He had spiritual wealth enough and to spare to pay his debt. Paul had more reasons than any of us to grumble. He was hounded, stoned, imprisoned, beaten, tried unjustly, and abandoned by friends. He was lonely, hungry, shipwrecked, laughed at, homeless, and helpless. But the only thing he grumbled about was the fact that there weren't enough hours in the day to tell people about his Savior and Lord and to build his church! The Bible is a treasury full of such models of people who have refused to hang up their joy on the gripe tree.

Resist self-pity.

Who of us have not felt sorry for ourselves for such trifling reasons as waiting in a long line at the checkout counter in the grocery store (why doesn't the woman in front of me pay cash, and why does she have one hundred coupons?). We can have a great pity party when the weather's bad—especially while we're on vacation. If we're women, we can gripe when we're having a bad hair day (you men if you're having a no-hair day). We can feel a gripe coming on if we find the car empty of gas in twenty-below-zero weather or if we are living alone and something needs to be fixed and there's no one there to fix it. Some of us feel put upon when we're treated unfairly or our work isn't respected or appreciated. Others mumble or grumble when they're left out.

We learn to gripe and have pity parties during those smaller, daily annoyances, but self-pity can develop during more tragic times, too. A good friend of mine spiraled into self-pity after her husband died suddenly on the mission field. She found herself asking why *her* husband had to die when there were so many selfish men in the world who could have died instead!

Seeing God's Hand Wherever We Are

Joseph is a great example to us when it comes to avoiding self-pity. He could very understandably have had a pity party, but he refused. Joseph, the eleventh son of Jacob, was favored and pampered (Gen. 37:3). His brothers became insanely jealous of him. One day he was sent by his father into the fields, where his siblings were tending sheep, to see how they were doing. The brothers, watching Joseph approach, plotted to rid themselves of him for good. They grabbed him and threw him into a water cistern that fortunately was empty.

It was literally the pits! Joseph's heart must have been thumping against his ribs. He heard his brothers arguing about how they were going to kill him, and he begged them to spare his life (Gen. 42:21). His shouts and tears did nothing but bring harsh words down on his head.

Joseph's hurt and shock must have been unbelievable. The whole thing was a living nightmare. He must have wondered incredulously how his own brothers could hate him so much. And then suddenly he heard strange and frightening voices.

The harsh voices grew louder and louder, and then his brothers were hauling him out of the pit. Joseph's great relief turned abruptly to terror as he was roughly tied up and handed over to Midianite slave traders. How did he feel as he watched, as if in a dream, while twenty pieces of silver changed hands? They were actually selling him like an animal! When that was over, the camels took off, carrying him away from his brothers. They soon disappeared from sight. Here he was on the way to Egypt to the slave market—or as far as he knew, to his death—and he was only seventeen (Gen. 37:2, 25-29).

You could say that Joseph had a dysfunctional family. Now, that's a reason to have a pity party! Don't you think it's a little unusual for big brothers to sell their little brothers into slavery (though some of them, if they were honest, would have to admit this thought had crossed their minds on occasion)? What a desperate situation—to find himself a victim at such a tender age, a piece of meat in the Egyptian market of human misery, far from his beloved parent and all that he held most dear.

God is in the pit, and God is in the prison, too! You can't keep him out of the pits and prisons of life.

Joseph was bought by Potiphar, who was an important official of Pharaoh. And Joseph was put to work. He who had been served by slaves as his father's favored son now slaved for others and their favored sons. He was subjected to sexual harassment and found himself in deep trouble for his godly stand; he was put in prison (Gen. 39).

Surely this was prime time for Joseph to have a pity party—to hang up his harp on the gripe tree! But Joseph saw that God was in the situation. God is in the pit, and God is in the prison, too! You can't keep him out of the pits and prisons of life.

And God had plans for Joseph that he was about to put into motion. Surely, as Joseph was to realize much later, "no plan of God's can be thwarted." In the end, God helped Joseph interpret dreams for Pharaoh, and Pharaoh released him from prison and gave him incredible honor. He also gave him authority, a home, and a wife (Gen. 41:41-45). Now he found himself, not in the pits or the prison, but in the palace! That's what God can do—if we dare to see his hand in our life rather than blind ourselves through negativity and griping.

Appreciating the pits—and the palaces

But the funny thing about all of this is that you'll never really appreciate the palace unless you've discovered what it means to handle the pits. Joseph handled himself in the palace with as much integrity as he had during his lowest moments. Even though Joseph ended up ruling Egypt, he was always a slave, a favored servant of Pharaoh. But this slave had a dream that he never allowed to die, a dream of using whatever pit, prison, or palace he happened to be in first and foremost for God's glory. He chose to be God's slave and serve him faithfully.

Joseph sang his song to the Babylonians (Egyptians in his case) and didn't allow any root of bitterness to stop him. He forgave his brothers, the Egyptians, and even the slave traders (Gen. 50:19-20). He apparently never bore a grudge and learned the secret of being content in any and every circumstance. He said to his brothers, "You intended to harm me, but God intended it for good to accomplish what is now being done, the saving of many lives" (v. 20).

We see the hand of God moving in a mysterious way in the story of Esther also. In Esther's day, God (knowing all things everywhere) was well aware that the Jewish race would face extermination through a Jew hater named Haman. However, in God's providence he moved a beautiful woman into a place of influence to rescue her people. Circumstances such as these are not happenstance in the economy of God. He is in control when we are out of control. But in the examples of Joseph and Esther we see that God had the whole thing in his hands all the time. It helps me to turn to stories like these in the Bible when it seems God is nowhere to be seen in my own pits, prisons, or palaces, and encourage myself. Sometimes it helps to pray a prayer like this:

> Lord, it's all so confusing—but you are not confused. Lord, it's all so dark—yet you are light. Lord, I read in Isaiah 40:27 that your people often complained: "My way is hidden from the Lord; my cause is disregarded by my God." Yet you reminded them in verse 28 that you are "the everlasting God, the Creator of the ends of the earth." If you hold the universe in place, you can hold me together, too. Thank you. Amen.

The Content of Contentment

Our life does not have to be in such turmoil as Joseph's or Esther's for us to be discontented and griping. One thing that can get us griping so that we lose our joy is not crisis but comparisons. These usually be-

gin with the words *if only.* Think of the Israelites. They lamented: "If
only we were back in Jerusalem!" "If only" is the language of discontent. If only I lived there instead of here, I'd be happy. If only I was
pretty, sporty, or clever like so-and-so. Or, if only I was married. Then,
if only I wasn't married! (Someone said that marriage is like a be-
sieged city—everyone inside is trying to get out, and everyone outside is trying to get in!) "If only I had a baby," lamented a woman who
was struggling with infertility. She found she was comparing herself
to her classmates, who all seemed to be pregnant. She had never sus-
pected that she could not get pregnant when she wanted and how she
wanted. As a result, she lost her joy. "If only I had a more interesting
job—like my best friend," complained another woman. But contentment isn't dependent on outside circumstances (good or bad), on
men or women, jobs, or even having children. I have come to believe
that the content of contentment is Christ.

The apostle Paul loved to talk about himself as a slave of Jesus
Christ. He, of all the apostles, found himself in many foreign lands
during his lifetime. He, like Joseph, had been in many pits, prisons, and palaces and through it all had sung a song of joy and contentment. Paul found the secret of his joy and generously shared it
with all of us: He learned that contentment is learned! It is an art. It
can be accomplished if practiced like any other art. It is not a gift,
the result of a particular personality trait, or a lucky gene. Neither
does it fall from heaven. It requires us to be in the school of life and
adversity in order to do our part. As we cooperate with God when
trouble troubles us, contentment begins to blossom in the garden
of our life. This is very encouraging to me. It means that anybody
can learn to be content—if he puts his mind to it and is willing.

Contentment can be a learned art.
It begins with the belief that God is in control
when you're out of it.

Many people believe contentment is a feeling—and you can't learn a feeling. Yet, contentment isn't primarily a feeling. It is a spiritual environment, a state of being—an ordering of our internal chaos: Contentment is inner peace. Augustine defined peace as the "tranquillity of order," and in a sense that is what contentment is. However, peace and contentment are not the absence of outward conflict but rather peace in the middle of conflict—tranquillity in the storm! Contentment isn't getting your own way either; it's a settled peace when you don't get your own way!

One day Paul, who was in as much trouble as the Israelites of old, was in prison. He was living out his last days, stripped of every comfort we take so much for granted. Fettered to a guard, Paul testified to the fact he was quite content! Deprived of his freedom—possibly facing lions or sword, Paul penned words that centuries later shout with superb serenity. These are words that are really amazing. After all, most of us are not looking for contentment when all is well with our world and our soul, but when all is ill with both! When the apostle wrote Philippians 4, he was going through one of the darkest parts of his career. Yet, as my husband puts it, "Prisoner though he was, he was 'bound for joy'!" Paul found that the secret of happiness was not in his circumstances but in the loving God who had permitted those circumstances to happen. Paul was concerned the Philippians might think he was dependent upon their generous gifts for contentment and peace. He wanted them to know that in every situation Christ would help him to maintain an attitude of trust and confidence in him (Phil. 4:12-14).

As far as Paul was concerned, the content of contentment was Christ. He said it this way: "For to me, to live is Christ and to die is gain" (Phil. 1:21). He really didn't care very much what happened to him—not because he had given up hope or was depressed or suicidal, but because he counted both options (life or death) as wonderful! It's hard to hurt a man with such a resilient philosophy. It's called contentment.

But I notice to my relief that this same grace, this virtue, can be acquired! Paul says, "I have learned to be content whatever the circumstances" (Phil. 4:11). We are enrolled by a loving God in the school of hard knocks and are expected to learn our lessons well. We can all be home schooling ourselves in the art of being content.

Life's instructors

When Paul says, "I am instructed to be" (Phil. 4:12, KJV), the word is *memuemai* (instructed); this spoke of a pagan initiation rite into a secret society. "I know both how to run low and how to run over," said Paul. As I think back over my life, I remember many of my own instructors in the school of contentment who knew how to run low and how to run over. When my husband was on the road for months at a time, loneliness was my teacher, and I found God quite sufficient for my many lonely "nows." When I wore out trying to be both Mom and Dad to our three lively kids, perseverance taught me endurance and strangely enough gave me a settled sense of stillness that couldn't be jolted even by most unpleasant surprises that were definitely not on my agenda. I did indeed know God had initiated me through the door of adversity into his secret society of contentment.

> *I have learned to accept what God allows and to change what he empowers me to change.*

I remember, years ago when we lived in England, putting my children to bed one night. My husband was in Australia—literally the other side of the world. He wasn't coming home for three long, hard months. My father had been diagnosed with cancer, my daughter had fallen and broken her arm the day my husband left, and my hands were more than full, running a preschool during the day and programs for dozens of needy teenagers in the evenings. (During this time it didn't help to catch mumps from my kids either!) Yet as I sat by the crackling fire in our tiny home, a huge sense of well-being invaded every corner of my life. I could hardly stand it. My heart was singing, and my soul was dancing. I was content.

I have learned to accept what God allows and to change what he empowers me to change; and that's usually my own attitude. I try to turn to Christ to meet my needs, be they physical, relational, or spiritual. He has always come through for me!

Years ago I stopped looking to anyone else but God to satisfy me. I have learned to be content with such things as I have, for he has said that he will never leave me nor forsake me (Heb. 13:5). There is no man that can love me enough, no child that can need me enough, no job that can pay me enough, and no experience that can satisfy me enough! Only Jesus. The compass of my life must be set in his direction and by his direction, and then it will, like a real compass, not be affected by movement!

Evidence of discontent

Tell me, to whom do you look when you feel there's a void in your life? Whose phone numbers do you dial, or whose fax numbers do you use? Where do you lean when you're in doubt or debt or depression or when death threatens? What things do you plan to accumulate to fill the needy needs of your heart? Where do you plan to go on vacation, or whom do you hope to meet at a party? When do you plan to succeed—why, where, how? Perhaps we need to search our soul for honest answers to such questions. Once the honest answer is given to God, it's helpful to use a hymn to respond. A hymn such as "Jesus, Lover of My Soul":

> *Jesus, Lover of my soul,*
> *Let me to Thy bosom fly,*

While the nearer waters roll,
While the tempest still is high.
Hide me, O my Savior, hide,
Till the storm of life is past;
Safe into the haven guide;
O receive my soul at last!

Other refuge have I none;
Hangs my helpless soul on Thee;
Leave, ah! leave me not alone,
Still support and comfort me.
All my trust on Thee is stayed,
All my help from Thee I bring;
Cover my defenseless head
With the shadow of Thy wing.

Thou, O Christ, art all I want;
More than all in Thee I find;
Raise the fallen, cheer the faint,
Heal the sick, and lead the blind.
Just and holy is Thy name,
I am all unrighteousness;
False and full of sin I am,
Thou art full of truth and grace.

Plenteous grace with Thee is found,
Grace to cover all my sin;
Let the healing streams abound;
Make and keep me pure within.
Thou of life the Fountain art,
Freely let me take of Thee;
Spring Thou up within my heart,
Rise to all eternity.
—Charles Wesley (1738)

Contentment and the will of God

We must be in the will of God to be content. When you believe you are exactly where God wants you to be, you won't be happy anywhere else in the whole wide world! Even if you feel you are sitting by the waters of Babylon as the Israelites were, you should know you cannot be truly happy outside the will of God. When we lay our complaints down about his workings in our life, we will be held together inside. In fact, the dictionary defines contentment as "to hold in or contain together"!

As I struggled as a young wife with being content with a husband who traveled a lot, I realized I would only be fully content if I and he were in the center of God's will. Since I believed it was God's will for Stuart to be doing what he had been called and commissioned to do, I knew I would not be happy if he were home! That mental acceptance helped my heart to begin its journey toward the peace I had been seeking. Peace of heart and mind, after all, is not dependent on a person but on being in the center of God's calling on your life. Therein lies peace and therein lies an inner cohesiveness that only the Holy Spirit can engineer.

> *Peace of heart and mind, after all, is not dependent on a person but on being in the center of God's calling on your life.*

What's going on inside you? Are you sitting under the gripe tree griping? Are you holding together or are you falling apart? When we are content with the choices God makes for us, we can respond rightly to everything life throws at us in all its shades and shadows. In other words, when we say a loud YES to God's decisions for us, we will find ourselves content! In fact the word *aye* (yes) is used in the British House of Commons as an affirmation vote. It has often been hard for me to glance heavenward and say aye to God's plans and purposes for my life. But a life of saying "yes, Lord" makes it easier to accept God's noes when they come. So to be content, we must determine to stay in the will of God, accepting what the will of God allows.

Remember the goal: sharing Christ.

There are certain principles we can usually follow to know if we are in God's will, to know that we're on track, such as: Have I been convinced in the past that this is God's calling for me? Has God given me any indication that he has changed his mind or his plans? People sometimes need some markers along the way to be sure that they are in tune with the will of God.

ONE MARKER IS THE DIRECTION WE SENSE AS WE READ THE WORD OF GOD.   Isaac Watts said, "Do not confuse yourselves with obscure and confused ideas." The Word of God will help us think straight about our unrealistic dreams, which may never materialize. The Scriptures remind us that "a man's life does not consist in the abundance of his possessions" (Luke 12:15). Paul was happy enough with what he had and didn't desire one thing more or less to feel complete.

WE MUST BE IN THE WORD OF GOD AND REFUSE TO LISTEN TO SATAN'S DARK AND SINISTER SUGGESTIONS.   Satan wants to confuse us as to the matter of contentment. We must refuse to listen to Satan, but rather bathe ourselves in Scripture.

WE MUST DECIDE TO BE MORE CONCERNED WITH THE CONCERNS OF GOD THAN WITH OUR OWN AFFAIRS.   The way to do this is to think of how Jesus was more concerned with our affairs than his own and try to follow his example. Look at the Cross, and think about how Jesus laid down his own ambitions in order to save us.

By constantly applying the example of the Cross to his ambitions and to his tendency to complain, Paul determined to look on the bright side of things and set his mind on winning others to the peace and forgiveness he had found in the Lord Jesus

Christ. Paul knew how to be content whether he was full or empty, rich or poor, rejected or accepted, loved or hated, followed or opposed, beaten or bandaged, stoned or worshiped, clothed or stripped naked, safe or in peril, tired out or well rested, burdened or light. He was content, believe it or not, to be either dead or alive! He was willing for all or nothing as long as God was there and God was using him. Paul, full of the Spirit, gave God permission to use him to his glory, and with that he was content—whatever the repercussions. The word used in Philippians 4 for *abased* denotes a voluntary acceptance of a lowly station, even poverty for Christ's sake. Some have suggested Paul was disinherited upon his becoming a Christian (1 Cor. 4:10-13; 2 Cor. 6:10). When things were chaotic or he suffered loss, Paul experienced Augustine's "tranquillity of order," because he was looking for ways to use the situation to lead people to Christ and not to make things more comfortable for himself.

For example, the guards he was chained to got to hear the gospel. After all, they were a captive audience! It makes you wonder who was the prisoner! After all, Paul believed with all his heart that the present problems he was enduring were the will of God for him. Prison or no prison, fetters or no fetters, "the things that had happened to him were falling out to the good of the gospel," and he was very happy about that! Contentment is finding the strength we need to accelerate the progress of the gospel—even when we are sitting in jail. Paul told us "in every circumstance" (literally, "everywhere and in all things") he was free and sufficient in Christ to care about other people's eternal well-being before his own physical, emotional, and even spiritual needs.

F. B. Meyer comments, "We can do a lot to elaborate the faculty of contentment; the germ of it is in our heart by the grace of God, but the flower and fruit demand our constant heed" (*The Epistle to the Philippians,* ed. 52, 2d ed. 56 [Marshall Morgan and Scott],

179). That's a tall order when we are in a prison of our own making or a victim of other people's sin, but then as Paul reminds us, "I can do everything through him who gives me strength" (Phil. 4:13).

There seem to be so many things to gripe about that contentment appears to be a pipe dream for many believers today. But it doesn't need to be—after all, it is the will of God that we find true contentment in him.

Griping as Negativity

The gripe tree holds the harps of those of us who not only react negatively to circumstances but who also have negative spirits by nature and do not apply the liberating power of God by his Spirit to our heart, our world, and its happenings. We often recite a long litany of misfortunes from as far back as we can remember. Then we look forward and list the misfortunes that are still sure to come. When these bad things do happen—perhaps as a result of our self-fulfilling prophecies—we say, "See, I knew it would happen!"

It's hard to know what comes first. Does a negative spirit spawn gripes, or does griping result in a negative spirit? Counting blessings helps. Underlining and memorizing Scripture promises helps, too. Believing the eternal is more important than the material will start us praising, and soon we'll be glorying in our infirmities, that the power of Christ may rest upon us, instead of griping about all our spiritual aches and pains! God hates the grumbler but gives grace to the thankful heart to sing a song of a fulfilled life to a grumbling and unhappy world.

George Beverly Shea's mother wrote the words to the song that George has sung around the world more times than any other song. When her son was twenty years old, she left the poem on his piano music rack, and he wrote the music that day. During the nearly nine years that Shea worked for the Mutual of New York Life Insurance Company, he continued his vocal training and singing in churches and for local Christian broadcasts. One day a director of a network radio station heard him sing and arranged for him to audition for a national program with the Lynn Murray Singers. Bev was thrilled with the prospect of singing on a network radio program, of being heard by large numbers of people, and of having a chance to make big money for a change. After passing the audition test, Bev Shea just didn't feel right about accepting this once-in-a-lifetime offer to be in secular work, so he declined. *No* was a strange word to such an offer, as positions such as these were rare during those Depression days, and thousands of young singers would have leaped at such an opportunity.

Whenever Bev Shea speaks to young people, his words of advice, based on the scriptural truths taught in Matthew 16:24-26, are usually these:

> God will always guide your life when you give the direction over to him. "If any man will come after me, let him deny himself, and take up his cross, and follow me. For whosoever will save his life shall lose it: and whosoever will lose his life for my sake shall find it. For what is a man profited, if he shall gain the whole world, and lose his own soul?" (Matt. 16:24-26, KJV)

Bev's favorite Scripture verse, one that he generally attaches to his signature, is found in Psalm 71:23: "My lips shall greatly rejoice when I sing unto thee; and my soul, which thou hast redeemed" (KJV). His signature hymn has been "I'd Rather Have Jesus." George Beverly Shea has surely found that the content of contentment is Christ!

> *I'd rather have Jesus than silver or gold,*
> *I'd rather be His than have riches untold;*
> *I'd rather have Jesus than houses or land,*
> *I'd rather be led by His nail-pierced hand:*
> *Than to be the king of a vast domain*

Or be held in sin's dread sway!
I'd rather have Jesus than anything
This world affords today.

I'd rather have Jesus than men's applause,
I'd rather be faithful to His dear cause;
I'd rather have Jesus than worldwide fame,
I'd rather be true to His holy name:
Than to be the king of a vast domain
Or be held in sin's dread sway!
I'd rather have Jesus than anything
This world affords today.

He's fairer than lilies of rarest bloom,
He's sweeter than honey from out the comb;
He's all that my hungering spirit needs—
I'd rather have Jesus and let Him lead:
Than to be the king of a vast domain
Or be held in sin's dread sway!
I'd rather have Jesus than anything
This world affords today.

LEARNING TO SING AGAIN

SPENDING TIME TOGETHER
For couples, families, Bible study groups, Sunday school classes, or for family devotions

1. Look up 1 Corinthians 10:6-12. Discuss verse 10. Does it surprise you that grumbling is included in the reasons that God destroyed these people? What does this tell you about God's attitude toward grumbling?

2. Read James 5:9. What command is there and why?

3. Read 1 Peter 4:9. What Christian service do we grumble about and why?

4. Read Philippians 4:12-14.

   - What convicts you?

   - What encourages you?

5. Pray together about the spirit of contentment needed

   - personally

   - corporately

   - in church matters

   - in the community

   - in the country

   - in the world

SPENDING TIME ALONE

1. Think of all the things that cause you to indulge in a pity party. Name them and confess them to God as sin.

2. Read Exodus 15:24 and Numbers 14:21-38. Note especially Numbers 14:24. What do you learn about

- God?

- the Israelites?

- Moses?

- yourself?

Pick out a verse that means something to you and memorize it.

3. Spend time in praise and thanksgiving, and ask God to help you guard against a murmuring spirit.

CHAPTER THREE

THE GRUDGE TREE

*And forgive us our sins—just as we forgive those
who have sinned against us.*

Luke 11:4, NLT

My husband abused me," said the woman. She sat blankly in front of me, seemingly empty of feeling. Then suddenly she began to talk and sob all at the same time. I listened to the sorry tale—one I have heard all too often. "I ended up in the hospital, my face battered and bruised." Instinctively she raised her hand to her cheek and whispered, "It's always the same—he comes home drunk." The description was vivid and moving. I felt her fear and found myself glancing out the window half anticipating her abusive spouse's sudden appearance. I wondered how I could help her. She obviously needed a safe place to go.

Then I noticed something that was incongruous. There was not a mark to be seen anywhere on her face, yet her description of the battering she had received had been so vivid I had believed it must have just occurred. "Forgive me for asking you," I said gently, "but I see no physical marks of abuse."

She looked at me, startled. "Oh," she said, "this happened twenty years ago!"

"But it didn't," I said, suddenly comprehending. "As far as you are concerned, it happened all over again today as you replayed the 'tape' for me. It happened again as you went to sleep last night and when you woke up this morning. And I expect it sometimes occurs in unexpected places as you glimpse a man in a crowd who resembles your husband. The memory tape plays continually, doesn't it?"

This poor woman was bearing a twenty-year-old grudge that was hurting her as much in the present as the physical battering had hurt her in the past.

Grudges can do that. They can bludgeon the sweetness and joy right out of your life, and you find yourself hanging up your joy on the grudge tree.

God's People Had a Grudge

The people of God knew all about losing the sweetness of life at the grudge (or vengeance) tree. Like the abused wife, they had been playing a mind movie of their past victimization over and over again. The vengeance video they played inside was destroying them in more complete ways than the torture they were going through at the hands of their enemies.

It's a killing thing, a slow suicide, to harbor unforgiveness and wrestle with a spirit of hatred.

It's a killing thing, a slow suicide, to harbor unforgiveness and wrestle with a spirit of hatred. The Lord says, "It is mine to avenge; I will repay" (Heb. 10:30). If we are honest, most of us who have been misused in some way can't help wanting to help the Lord out on payday! Unbelievers feel that vengeance is a valid response to anyone who has done them wrong. "Don't get mad; get even," Lee Iacocca is reputed to have advised his sons. But that is not the sort of parental advice a believer should give to his children. Yet here by this Babylonian river the Israelites were actually teaching their children this sort of attitude.

> O Daughter of Babylon, doomed to destruction, happy is he who repays you for what you have done to us. (Ps. 137:8)

When you can't sing a song of the Lord, better to stay silent than sing a grudge song! "Go on, sing us one of your God songs," taunted their captors. But the Israelites hung up their harps on the grudge tree and rendered a song of bitterness and hatred instead.

Dealing with Our Own Sin First

There is no way to sing a new song without deliberately tuning out the old song, and tuning out means repentance. Even if there is 99 percent culpability on the part of another, there will probably be one percent of something we need to own—something we either did do or didn't do. We can start by using the psalmist's words and by asking God to search us and know our heart; test our thoughts and point out anything he finds in us that makes him sad; and lead us along the path of everlasting life (Ps. 139:23, TLB).

I have also found it helpful, when I am struggling with righteous indignation or unrighteous anger, to get alone with the Lord and spend time focusing on my own sinfulness instead of someone else's. Other people's hymns and songs have been an incredible source of blessing at these times and have restored my perspective as I have returned to grapple with a relational problem. Hymns like M. Saward's:

> *Fire of God, titanic Spirit,*
> *Burn within our hearts today,*
> *Cleanse our sin; may we exhibit*
> *Holiness in every way.*
> *Purge the squalidness that shames us,*
> *Soils the body, taints the soul;*

And through Jesus Christ, who claims us,
Purify us; make us whole.

Wind of God, dynamic Spirit,
Breathe upon our hearts today,
That we may your power inherit,
Hear us, Spirit, as we pray.
Fill the vacuum that enslaves us,
Emptiness of heart and soul,
And through Jesus Christ, who saves us,
Give us life and make us whole.

Voice of God, prophetic Spirit,
Speak to every heart today,
To encourage or prohibit,
Urging action or delay.
Clear the vagueness which impeded us,
Come, enlighten mind and soul,
And, through Jesus Christ, who leads us,
Teach the truth that makes us whole.
—Keswick Praise (p. 77)

Confessing my own spiritual poverty and looking to him for a word of rebuke or instruction has been a place to begin when I've lost my joy. In other words, when I've hung up my harp, I can listen to someone else's harp strings! Personal prayer and repentance lead to renewal and joy. And our renewal leads to the renewal of others around us because it releases us to have a relationship with our enemies.

There is no question in my mind that the Israelites wanted spiritual renewal. But they wanted it on their own terms, without repentance, and it doesn't work that way. When you read Psalm 137, you sense that they felt no responsibility for their present dilemma. There is no hint they were mourning their rebel hearts. The pathway to joy, even when you're sitting by the waters of Babylon, lies in a willingness to recognize your own failures and trespasses and to confess them.

God's Forgiveness Helps Us Forgive

Every day in the English school system of which I was a part, we had a school assembly. We prayed the Lord's Prayer daily. I remember praying dutifully, "Forgive us our trespasses as we forgive those who trespass against us." I didn't have a clue as to the meaning of this worthy prayer! Now I know it means that I've hurt God by my thoughts, words, actions, and attitudes, but I can ask him to forgive me, and he promises he will. He does this because he doesn't hold grudges against the one who is sorry. Because he doesn't hold grudges, he doesn't want us to. The sense of that gracious forgiving act of God should birth a grateful response in us that helps us to extend forgiveness to people who have hurt us.

An ugly family story

"But you don't understand," my friend who had been abused said to me. "I didn't deserve this." "This" was the fact that it was her husband who had treated her so badly. "It was family. . . ." Her voice trailed away, and I found myself quoting aloud: "Remember, O Lord, what the Edomites did on the day Jerusalem fell. 'Tear it down,' they cried, 'tear it down to its foundations!'" (Ps. 137:7).

She looked at me uncomprehendingly, and I smiled and said, "Let me tell you a story." So I did. I told her about the Edomites. It had been the Babylonians who had smashed the baby Israelites against the rocks, but it was the Edomites who had cheered them on! The Edomites were related to Israel. The nation of Israel were descendants of Jacob, and the Edomites were descendants of his brother, Esau. They shared the land on their southern border, and when the Babylonians destroyed Jerusalem, the Edomites cooperated with the invaders who were plundering the city. The Israelites' sense of betrayal was incredible because this was "family" doing this to them.

"It's hard when it's your brother, your husband—your family—who abuses you, isn't it?" I said to my friend.

She nodded, understanding the application. "But I can't stop playing the vengeance video!" She sobbed bitterly.

"You can stop reminding yourself," I said. "Playing the vengeance tape is a way of reminding yourself of a great betrayal. There will be few bright moments in your soul if you choose to go on putting that tape in your mind machine! One of the secrets of beginning to forgive is in realizing we are just as much a sinner, in other respects, as the other person. That's a hard pill to swallow."

Attitudes Lead to Actions

On one occasion Jesus taught that attitudes lead to actions. Anger, for instance, is the root from which the fruit of killing comes. Sin is sin; it's all the same in God's eyes. Murder is hatred taken to its logical conclusion. The Babylonians hated Israel, but in God's eyes the Israelites' hatred of their enemies was just as much sin as the Babylonians' hatred.

Bridget*had a cousin who was twenty-one years of age. She had two beautiful kids—a three-year-old and an eleven-month-old baby. Nearby a foster child was growing up. His mother had been put in a mental institution when he was born, and he had lived in a series of foster homes since. This disturbed young man, who lived at a nearby farm, began to act very strangely. He killed an animal at the farm and skinned it! One day the dog he was very fond of died, and the young man became very agitated. When this seventeen-year-old knocked on Bridget's cousin's door, she welcomed the boy into their house. He was familiar—a friend, almost family. But that day that young man took out a knife and stabbed Bridget's cousin to

*Names have been changed to protect the family's privacy.

death—then the three-year-old and the eleven-month-old. He was arrested, tried, convicted, sentenced, and sent to prison.

Bridget had come to faith six years previously. She was now in Christ, a new creation. She was a single parent raising a young boy with her own issues to work through, without the murder of a loved cousin and her infant children on top of it all. Before she knew Christ, it would have been easy. She would have regarded the murderer as the rest of the world did—evil and without hope.

Her reaction to the young murderer, who had butchered part of her family as he had butchered the animal at the farm, was at first horror, then righteous anger—and who could blame her? But now that she was "in Christ," she found herself praying for the young murderer. "If he could just find you as his Savior," she prayed to the Lord. And then incredibly he did! Now he, too, was in Christ. He had become her "brother"!

Bridget became involved in prison ministries. In her words, she now had a problem, for she realized that she who had been reconciled to God had now been given a ministry of reconciliation. It took three years to struggle with the turmoil in her heart, and still she wasn't quite sure she could forgive the boy. "I knew I wouldn't know if I'd really forgiven him," she told me, "until I held him in my arms and told him I loved him." Another year and a half passed before Bridget asked for and received permission to visit the boy, along with the prison chaplain.

They talked together for a long time. At last Bridget stood up, put her arms around the young man, and simply said, "I love you." Then she said, "I have no right to judge you. All my sins, though very different from your sins, are just as great in the sight of God."

"I have no right to judge you. All my sins, though very different from your sins, are just as great in the sight of God."

"Meeting him," she told me, "changed my whole life."

Some of those changes weren't all good either. Not everyone understood her actions. Tough things were said to her; close relationships were broken because of it. But time tempers things, and healing has begun in some other broken hearts because of her obedience. Bridget believes obedience is the first step toward reconciliation. She believes God directed her to that rendezvous. She had a choice to turn up for the interview or back out. Bridget testified to an "incredible" compassion flooding her soul as that young man, who had changed the lives of a family forever, walked into the room at the prison. Now, in truth, she didn't regard him from a worldly point of view anymore; he was not a monster but a boy. *This could be my own son,* she thought. This woman realized that she had had radical spiritual heart surgery. Now she served one who had told her he wanted her to forgive as she had been forgiven. He who said, "Love your enemies" now dominated her thinking and began to influence her behavior.

Now Ministers of Reconciliation

Once we have been reconciled to God, he gives us the ministry of reconciliation. We become his ambassadors, speaking on his behalf. He changes our life, so we can be the instruments in his hands to bring his saving, changing power to others! He won't ask any of us to do exactly the same thing Bridget did (aren't you glad about that!), but he will ask us all to be obedient and to forgive as we have been forgiven, demonstrating it in a thousand different ways as the opportunity comes.

There came a point when the Israelites had to face their enemies, and they had an opportunity to forgive them. Face-to-face with their tormentors, they had the chance to admit that all sin is sin and that rebellion against God was a terrible sin because of their spiritual privileges. It was much greater than the sin of the lost Gentiles, who had had little or no light on the matters of God. God's people had a chance, as Bridget did, to put their arms around the people who had grievously wronged them and tell them they loved them—or at least sing them a love song from the Lord. But they missed it. They were too busy festooning the shrubbery with their silent harps!

Who Is the Edomite in Your Life?

Is there an Edomite you need to forgive? An ex-spouse, an angry child, an estranged family member? Perhaps a boss, a colleague, or someone else has wronged you. Perhaps one of your children is in trouble, and you are having a terrible time forgiving the one who brought the trouble into his or her life.

> *How can you forgive someone who doesn't ask or want to be forgiven?*

And what if the offending party hasn't asked to be forgiven? How can you forgive someone who doesn't ask or want to be forgiven, someone who has no intention of acknowledging any wrongdoing? A verse of Scripture helped me in this regard. "If your brother sins, rebuke him, and if he repents, forgive him" (Luke 17:3). If an attempt to confront him has failed to elicit a response and Scriptures have been rejected—then what?

Staying in "ready" mode

Jesus told a story in Luke 15 about a prodigal son who abused all his family privileges. He claimed his inheritance ahead of time and took off to waste it all by living a flagrantly rebellious life. After finding himself bankrupt and deserted by his fair-weather friends—who had no compunction in helping him to spend his fortune—he ended up starving in a pigsty, looking after pigs. (This was about as far away as a good Jewish boy could get from his roots; Jews don't eat pork!) Meanwhile his loving, grieving father climbed to the flat roof of his house to watch for his son's return.

When he finally came to his senses, he said to himself, "At home even the hired men have food enough and to spare, and here I am, dying of hunger! I will go home to my father and say, 'Father, I have sinned against both heaven and you, and am no longer worthy of being called your son. Please take me on as a hired man.'" (Luke 15:17-19, TLB)

As soon as the ragged figure appeared on the horizon, the waiting father ran down that long road of repentance to meet him, greet him, clothe him, feed him, restore him, and—grace upon grace—*forgive* him.

> *Forgiveness has great vision,*
> > *sharpened by stern exercise.*
> *Daily he's found scanning hope's*
> > *horizon,*
> *willing a dear familiar figure into sight.*

> *And when at last he sees his son,*
> > *limping toward home,*
> *Forgiveness doesn't grab a bull horn and*
> > *start yelling orders—*

> *"Down on your knees, boy,*
> > *you'll pay for the pain*
> > *you've caused*
> > *your brother and me—*
> > *grovel first—grace next."*

> *Because Forgiveness knows full well the*
> > *penitent's purse is a barren wallet of want*
> > *unable to birth payment*
> > *for past sin.*

Crushed against his Father's heart
   salt on his lips—the child
   lays down the works of grief at his Father's feet
   "I'm sorry—I'm so sorry,
   I was so wrong."

Joy in heaven! Angels' laughter
   wakes the birds at midnight
   sure that it is dawn!

The Father digs a deep grave for
   the past and
   leaves the death of love
   behind.

The present waits—
   January—transfigured
   by apple blossoms—
   miracle of life!

Dressed for the feast
   the fatted calf
   awaits
   the celebration.
THE MASTER'S SON IS HOME!
—J. B.

I am learning to try to keep myself on "standby," as the father in the story did, watching for the return, straining my "prayer eyes" in the direction of the wandering one. But I am also conscious that the father did not take off down the road to the pigsty, burst in on his boy's privacy, and pronounce, "I forgive you." Repentance had to come first. As I have waited for such a reunion, I have tried to stay in a "welcome home" mode in my heart while giving freedom for people to choose their actions. We must give people the option for reconciliation. They have God-given freedom to choose, but they don't have the freedom to choose the repercussions of those choices. Those consequences play themselves out in their lives. Meanwhile we wait, asking God to keep us in a ready-to-run-down-the-road state of heart and mind. Harboring a grudge makes this open attitude impossible. We need to talk to the Lord about that! Getting rid of the grudge clears the way for redemption's response.

I have tried to stay in a "welcome home"
mode in my heart while giving freedom for people
to choose their actions.

Years ago my husband accompanied a missionary who was visiting a primitive tribe. The only "hotel" in the jungle village happened to be under the open straw dome of the village doctor (as in *witch* doctor!). Lying on the floor, my husband asked the missionary what the various objects festooning the ceiling were. "That's the old fellow's accounting system," replied the missionary. "Those objects represent real or perceived wrongs that people in the village have done to the old 'doc' or his family. He would feel really disloyal if he forgot these grievances, so he hangs these things up so he can go to sleep keeping count." My husband marveled at this. This man was keeping a running record of everyone's sins!

For those of us who count ourselves civilized, this sounds either ludicrous (and good reason to send missionaries to the foreign field) or it rings a bell! Perhaps the old witch doctor isn't so very different from us. What, I wonder, do we have hanging around the roof of our mind? What running record are we keeping and on whom? When we lie down to sleep, what are we deliberately keeping in our mind's eye?

God, our loving heavenly Father, doesn't keep an account of our sins. First Corinthians 13:5 says: "Love does not demand its own way. It is not irritable or touchy. It does not hold grudges and

will hardly even notice when others do it wrong" (TLB). God, who
is love, stands willing to forgive and forget everything we've done
or will do the moment we ask him to. He doesn't pronounce us forgiven, however, until we ask him to! He waits like the father in the
story—loving, hoping, looking, and waiting for the first footstep
on the road back home. At that first step, you will find him running
down the road toward you, and after your "Father, forgive me,"
you will hear his great glad cry: "This son of mine was dead and is
alive again; he was lost and is found" (Luke 15:24).

I well remember lying in my bed at the age of fourteen, looking at
a Bible on my bookshelf. I was not a believer, and I had no idea whose
old Bible it was. There it lay among all my other teenage reading. A
little voice from somewhere said to me, "Pick it up, open it, read it."
But I resisted. There was, however, born in my fourteen-year-old
heart that day a longing to obey that still small voice—to reach out
and take those worn pages in my young hands, smooth down the
brown edges, and read it! It was a full five years later that Jill Ryder
started out—barefoot and dirty—down that long road of repentance
into my Father's arms. But as I look back, I believe the angels started
practicing a song of praise to sing right then and there. And somehow
I believe my loving, giving, gracious heavenly Father said to them,
softly, "Look, she's coming home!"

It brings me to tears to think about that first "sorry" step I took
that night, and it brings me to joy and gladness, glory, and praise to
think of the last one that landed me in the loving arms of God! I
never doubted my God's patience and grace with me, and I never
for a moment believed he would not be there waiting when at last I
arrived at the Cross. Having abused my privileges, wasted my life
with rebellious living, grieved my parents, and disgraced my God,
I was not disappointed at my homecoming.

And now as his forgiven, restored child, I know as he forgave
me, so I must forgive the Edomites and Babylonians in my life. I
must be ready; I must be waiting; I must be patient and full of grace

like he was for me. I have found that grace and grudges cannot live together!

So watch with the Father. Climb often to the rooftop. Expect God to answer your prayers, and have a plan of action ready. Decide on what you'll say or what you'll do to show the one "coming home" you mean your statements of forgiveness.

The father in Jesus' story covered up what he could with a robe. He didn't needlessly expose the son's rags. He didn't demand he walk into the palace without provision. He gave him a ring—indicating the boy's relationship to him—and he worked at helping others who had been hurt by his rebellious boy's behavior to also receive him back.

I wonder if any Babylonians were sorry for their tormenting? I wonder if any responded to Isaiah's ministry and asked the Israelites to forgive them? We know that many masters have been won to faith by their slaves. How many Israelites prayed for their enemies? Who among the slave drivers heard an early version of the prayer Jesus prayed centuries later: "Father, forgive them, for they know not what they do" or Stephen's "Lay not this sin to their charge"? Only heaven will tell. Meanwhile we can practice our songs in readiness for our own relational challenges that lie ahead.

Are You under the Grudge Tree?

How do we know when we're holding a grudge? What kinds of feelings or behavior in ourselves do we experience when we haven't forgiven someone? Do any of these statements apply to you?

- When I hear this person's name, my stomach knots up and my mood changes for the worst.

- If I know that a certain person will be at a party, I find a reason not to attend.

- I've stopped praying for this person. I'm really not very concerned about him or her.

- Sometimes I realize that I'm "telling off" this person in imaginary conversations, and as I imagine it, I'm getting angry all over again.

- I find that I feel a little bit of satisfaction when things don't go well for that person.

It's time to take these thoughts and feelings to the waiting room, confess to God that we have a lack of forgiveness, and allow him to work forgiveness in our heart.

How to Sing under the Grudge Tree

Finding forgiveness

When it's *my* turn to "fess up" to the fact that something is my fault, I discover that my old self rises quickly to its feet to defend my actions. The flesh will give every excuse in the book before it will say, "I was wrong—please forgive me." I find that it helps me to get off to a quiet place with my Bible and just read. Sometimes I'll read a whole book before I'll start to pray.

It's a lot more important for God to talk to us than for us to talk to him! So I invite him to do just that. Invariably a phrase or verse, parable or quote will hit me between the eyes because it has relevance to my exact need.

I remember bossing around someone who had been put on a work team with me. I was conscious of a cool response from this friend; she muttered, "I like to be asked, Jill, not told!" I was taken aback and ignored her rejoinder, but when I was alone, I thought about her words. "I am such a controller, Lord," I confessed. "Gentle me with the Spirit's sweet grace. Help me to be a servant and not 'lord it over others—as the Gentiles do.' Make me sensitive. Help me listen to myself talking and giving orders. Temper my strong personality with the Spirit's gentleness."

Then I went to find my friend and offered an apology, which she accepted lovingly, and we prayed about it.

That prayer together, of course, is an essential ingredient if we are to see our relationships mended. Somehow you can't harbor resentment when you're on your knees together at the foot of the cross—it just doesn't work!

My biggest problem sometimes is calling things by their proper names. When someone else gets appreciated or someone else's book wins an award, and I complain, asking myself why she got noticed instead of me—especially when I think I've done as much or as well as she has—I need to drag that proud attitude out into the light of God and call it what it is: jealousy!

Most jealousy is lack of real love—love that is more interested in the other's well-being, irrespective of cost to myself. In some way, any sin of attitude or action I commit against another person is actually my failure to love them as God does. For this lack of love, we must ask God's forgiveness.

Offering forgiveness

Once Jesus used a story to teach forgiveness. He told a parable of a man in debt who was forgiven by his master; the master assumed the loss caused by the offender. When I read that, I realized I needed to do the same. There was someone I had to forgive. I needed to quit holding them liable for the wrong they had done to me; I needed to assume the loss and go on from there.

This process happened internally, when I was on my knees before God. I couldn't offer the offender forgiveness until it was asked for, but I could stay in a waiting mode and forgive, whether there would be any reconciliation or not. I did find out that forgiveness is not a done deal—a onetime thing. A photograph or a piece of music that brought back painful memories would start my stomach churning. A letter tucked away or a piece of artwork given to me for a birthday present by the person would summon her face before my mind's eye. A movie we'd seen together—even favorite flowers we shared in common—could trigger the hurtful memories, and things I had believed forgiven and forgotten would spring far too readily to mind. Then I would need to internally deal with the rising resentment all over again.

I like that word peacemaker. *It's been my experience that peace doesn't just happen; it's made.*

After praying about your hurt and giving it up, you'll find yourself free to pursue reconciliation. It might not be possible, but it's worth a try—for your own heart's good. Write a note offering to meet for coffee, or begin a correspondence. Sometimes writing is easier than talking for both parties. I find that the hardest obstacle to overcome is the first time you meet after there has been a severing of a relationship. It's hard to look the person in the face, but you must at least try. It helps to have a couple of things ready to say. For example, you could rehearse such phrases as "Thanks for coming; I really appreciate it" or "I admire you for making this effort, and I'm really thankful." I find that it's good to meet in a restaurant. Food helps—as a distraction that can ease the halting conversation or cause a diversion if things are getting difficult. I have to say my stomach is usually in such a knot that I can't eat very well at such times, but at least I can toy with the food!

Sometimes it's best to take the initiative in the conversation—at least you need to be prepared to—especially if you're the offended party. You can say something like, "I'm excited to be here because I've hated what's happening between us. Maybe we can get some things cleared up." It's a good idea to kick the dialogue off by admitting to a wrong you can legitimately own in the situation. You can always find something that you can be sorry about—even if you have to say, "I'm sorry that I haven't been sorry enough about what happened to do this before now." Don't be disappointed if you don't become buddy-buddy again the first time you meet. It could take many lunches and more prayers and initiatives than you'd like to think about before your relationship is restored. Perhaps your relationship will never be as it was before the trouble, but that's OK, too. It's enough to get what you can. At least you'll know that you made a valiant effort to be the peacemaker.

I like that word *peacemaker*. It's been my experience that peace doesn't just happen; it's made. And it's often made by the person who has had their personal peace shattered by another party. One thing I do know. I get my joy back when I've tried to bridge the chasm of shattered relationships. There is a peace that comes with the realization that God knows what a huge effort it took for me to take the first step forward, even if the person takes another step backward or rejects my efforts altogether. At least I know he knows I did my level best—and somehow my heart begins to sing again.

LEARNING TO SING AGAIN

SPENDING TIME TOGETHER
For couples, families, Bible study groups, Sunday school classes, or for family devotions

1. Fill in the acrostic. What are the characteristics of a grudge?

- G
- R (e.g., remembering)
- U
- D
- G
- E

Fill in the acrostic. What are the countering characteristics of God's grace?

- G
- R
- A (e.g., acceptance)
- C
- E

2. Why was it hard for the Israelites to forgive the Edomites? Why is it hard for us to forgive others?

3. Read Luke 15:11-31. There were really two prodigals in this story: the one who wouldn't stay home and the one who wouldn't leave home to look for him! Discuss the older son, who was bearing a grudge.

- Why do you think he was bearing a grudge?

- How does a grudge behave? How does it talk?

- What does the Father think about grudges?

- What action did the son need to take?

SPENDING TIME ALONE

1. Look through a hymnbook for a song about forgiveness—or use the one on pages 47–48. Sing it to God and to an Edomite. (Copy and send it or put it in your own words in a letter. If you have a nice voice, sing it to him/her!)

2. Spend time waiting on the Lord and thinking about this. Read some of these passages of Scripture that talk about God's faithful forgiveness. Let these words "talk" to you; then you talk to him about them.

- Lamentations 3:19-26

- Luke 23:32-43

3. In prayer, think about the joy of the Lord you used to have. Where did you lose it? If it was at the grudge tree, why not "return" to that place in your mind and ask God to deal with it.

- Tell him you don't want to harbor a grudge.

- Tell him specifically which grudge—about what/who— you're talking about. (This is not because he needs to know; he needs to hear you articulate the specifics.)

- Own and confess any part you had in causing the action against you. (If there is none that you can see, tell him.)

- Ask him to release you from the grip of the grudge.

- Thank him that he has heard and will do so in days ahead.

- Ask him if you should take any action contacting the people concerned. If so, what? (As you wait, expect some ideas to come to your mind, unless you know perfectly well what you need to do.) Share a prayer need concerning this with a trusted friend. Notice this idea is at the end of the list and not the beginning!

CHAPTER FOUR

THE GROWTH TREE

*He gives strength to the weary and increases
the power of the weak.*
Isaiah 40:29

W hat do you want to be when you grow up?" I asked a five-year-old boy. He looked at me, solemnly, thinking hard. Suddenly he grinned and with a flash of inspiration replied, "Bigger, I want to be bigger!" This was an understandable desire for a little chap with three older siblings. It's no fun always being on the bottom of the pile.

He was thinking in physical terms, of course, while I was thinking in terms of vocation or calling. Growth occurs in so very many dimensions, doesn't it? Healthy, physical growth is a gift we healthy people hardly think about. It isn't until tragedy strikes and a child is left stunted or crippled or stops growing altogether that we recognize the incredible gift of life that brings growth.

And what about those who have stopped growing emotionally or socially? Our hospitals, clinics, and doctors' offices are full of patients desperately wanting to grow past self-inflicted loneliness, relational disasters, or personal pain.

Growth of a Soul

Yet the most important dimension of human growth is in the area of spiritual life. The growth of a soul is far more important than the growth of a body, mind, or social calendar! Ask hundreds of Christians what they want to be when they grow up, and unfortunately few will tell you, "I want to be bigger spiritually"! Few will say, "My passion is to grow in God and expand my spiritual horizons."

No one would argue that most of us want to grow if it means experiencing more inner joy. Perhaps we first need to realize that there is no joy to be found in being spiritually stunted. Like the Israelites by the waters of Babylon, many Christians have hung up their harps on the growth tree.

Growing supposes knowing.

Knowing God comes before any real growth in our spirit. There's no knowing without experiencing for ourselves the person and presence of God and his Son, Jesus, through the Holy Spirit. It's a bit like knowing all about a different country but never really knowing it until you visit it. The Israelites knew all about Babylon but never knew it in stark, intimate reality until they were encamped by the river Chebar.

There's no knowing without experiencing for ourselves the person and presence of God and his Son, Jesus, through the Holy Spirit.

I remember a typically beautiful British autumn day in 1969 when my husband came cheerily into the house, joined us at the evening meal, and announced, "Well, kids, we're going to America!" The three children's eyes widened. David glanced a little nervously at his sister, who was staring into her cup. Pete cracked a joke (his way of relieving the tension in the situation), and my heart pumped furiously. What would it all mean for the Briscoe family? What would life hold for us all?

"I know about America," David offered. "We did it in school this year." It was true that David knew a little about America. He had been made aware of its existence through education. But awareness wasn't "knowing." In the months of preparation that lay ahead, Stuart (who was already traveling in the U.S.) would send us photographs or make wonderfully descriptive audiotapes, adding details to our knowledge. "They move houses on lorries—on the road?" Judy asked incredulously. "Dad likes walking round shops?" Pete commented in awe, after one tape where Stuart had discovered and described the American "malls." "These people have the most wonderful way of painlessly taking your money out of your pocket," was his father's comment.

Even as awareness wasn't knowing, information wasn't knowing either, but the more we became aware and gained information, the more we began to get excited about the real knowing that lay ahead. Dad brought baseball hats home, magnets for my refrigerator, and a Barbie doll for Judy. We felt really good about all that! But even our warm feelings about the U.S.A. did not constitute a true knowing.

Knowing is being there.

On November 11, 1970, we boarded a plane at a London airport and, with all our goods packed in two suitcases apiece, traveled with our golden retriever, Prince, to O'Hare Airport in Chicago, Illinois. Now at last the true knowing began! We had arrived! Knowing God is not awareness, information, or emotional stirrings. Knowing is *being there*. It involves getting on a plane of faith and leaving the past to lay hold of the future. It's actually arriving at your destination and beginning to investigate your new life. And that, of course, is only the beginning of the true knowing.

How Attitude Affects Growth

The Israelites really did know God. They had arrived at their destination years before when they had responded to God's initiative in calling them into a covenant relationship with him. The problem was that after really knowing him they stopped growing in him. Their stunted growth had a lot to do with attitude.

When I came to the States in 1970 for my husband's sake, my children's sake, and my own sake, I fixed my heart, soul, and mind in God and set out to explore and embrace my new environment. I watched my attitude carefully. I have found that this principle helps me whenever I find myself in a "foreign land." It's a question of focusing on God's will, fixing my mind on him, and facing the challenge with a good heart attitude. As Warren Wiersbe says, "We can either curse God and die, or trust God and grow."

Then it's a question of asking God, What do you want me to grow in the garden of my life? What fruit of Christlike character do you want to produce from the soil of this suffering or separation? For example, is it the flowers of love, joy, peace, or patience? In what way will I grow more like your Son, Jesus Christ, in this unexpected place? There is such joy in growing an herb garden of habits that honor the Lord or a rose garden of responsibilities we determine to fulfill or a shrubbery of shady trees to help a hot and weary traveler we might meet along the way. But if we hang up our harp on the growth tree, there will be no such music to be shared on our travels. So what causes us to stop growing?

Beware the mini-mind-set.
One type of bad attitude is pettiness, or small-mindedness. We may become just like the Israelites: jot-and-tittle people. All of us can fall into this trap. I constantly ask the Lord to keep me from having a mini-mind-set, from thinking small, below average. I'll never escape from this tendency because having a larger view demands something from me in terms of life effort, vision, personal education, and a whole lot of my valuable time. And by nature I'm lazy. Choosing to be maxi-minded instead of petty-minded results in my trying to make a significant difference where I live—to be salt, arresting corruption, and light in a dark place.

How does <u>pettiness</u> play itself out in our daily life? Well, we could say that pettiness worries about whether it's too hot or too cold while <u>he's sitting in a cushy church sanctuary</u>, whether someone took his spot in the church parking lot, or whether anyone noticed or acknowledged his latest contribution. And pettiness bites and devours his brothers who aren't as petty as he is! It's a great pity to turn into a jot-and-tittle person. We should not spend all our energy crossing our t's and dotting our i's. If we do, we will be small-impact people and may never sound Jesus' name freely and creatively on other people's heartstrings!

I constantly ask the Lord to keep me from having a mini-mind-set, from thinking small, below average.

One day Jesus listened to his disciples arguing about lunch! "Lift up your eyes," he advised them. "Look on the fields; they are white already to harvest." If we have our eyes fixed on the crumbs in our hands, we'll never see the one who grew the grain in the first place, even if he is standing in front of us. The hungry multitudes will never be fed if we find ourselves arguing about which bread is best—whole wheat or white! The Lord needs to deliver us from being so shortsighted and picky!

Pettiness can affect our attitude at home as well as abroad. When my teenage daughter and I were finding out how to live together and like each other, I found myself being picky about her manners, friends, language, and taste in clothes. One day she wanted to wear jeans to a church service. "That's not appropriate," I said. An argument ensued. Stuart walked into the room at the height of it and asked us what was the matter. We both laid out our case, and he looked at us thoughtfully. He then proceeded to tell us a story about Muhammad Ali. "He always let his coach pick his

Noar Scorpio

fights," he said. "I suggest you do the same. Ask yourselves, Is this worth a war? Is this a moral matter? In other words, pick your fights!" I took his advice. It saved me from wrecking my relationship with Judy. If you waste all your energy fighting about picky things, you'll have no energy left over to tackle the big issues that need to be worked out.

Pettiness is a stunting thing. It can hamper the growth of a soul more than many a "big" sin. The Song of Solomon reminds us that it's the "little foxes" that spoil the fruit in the vineyard! The little foxes of pettiness surely spoiled the fruit in the Israelites' lives and can spoil it in ours!

Beware of basic selfishness.

In the end it is my own selfish attitude that prevents me from growing up spiritually. Who can stop my growing? I can! In the final analysis, it is my sinful self—"the flesh," "the old man"—that I have been describing. It is my fallen nature that knows how to be hostile to God without anyone telling me how. It is the sin that spoiled me, that keeps God at arm's length, that backs off when serious sin needs forgiving or an entrenched habit must be faced and overcome. If I'm honest (and my sinful nature shudders at the thought), I don't want to be like Jesus; I want to be like me! That's the essence of the flesh. Worldliness is selfishness strutting its stuff. To see something is to want it; to want it is tantamount to having to have it. Self is all for getting, not giving; living, not dying; controlling, not releasing. What keeps Jill Briscoe from knowing God more intimately? Jill Briscoe!

In the same way, it was the Israelites' self-centered heart attitude that kept them from growing. It was their losing battle with their own sinful nature that did them in in the end, so that they hung up their harps in defeat.

Growth Comes from Feeding the Spirit

Amalek is a picture the Bible gives of the flesh nature. God had told his people to get rid of the Amalekites, a fierce enemy. He said his people were to have nothing to do with them. He warned that there would be hostility and warfare between them and the Israelites throughout their nation's life if they didn't wipe them out. When Israel was wandering around in the desert of sin, the Amalekites crept up behind them and picked off the sick and the weak, the old and the infirm. They knocked off the stragglers one by one. That's how Amalek works. The "old man" within us knows our weak spots; he bides his time and attacks us when we can least resist him. The answer, now as then, for all of us who would be "growing in our knowing" is to feed the soul and starve the flesh. We need to strengthen our weak spots and grow strong in the Holy Spirit.

How then do we feed the spirit within us and not the flesh? How and when in this frenetic world can we make a space for meaningful time with God? Each must decide the *whens* and *wheres* according to his or her particular circumstances. But if we would be holy—wholly his and holy his—we must take time. And there's the clue. It really isn't a question of making time but of taking time. We will need to take time from something else in order to engage in the most important thing. In the words of William Longstaff:

> *Take time to be holy, speak oft with thy Lord;*
> *Abide in Him always, and feed on His Word.*
> *Make friends of God's children; help those who are weak;*
> *Forgetting in nothing His blessing to seek.*
>
> *Take time to be holy, the world rushes on;*
> *Much time spend in secret with Jesus alone;*
> *By looking to Jesus, like Him thou shalt be;*
> *Thy friends in thy conduct His likeness shall see.*
>
> *Take time to be holy, let Him be thy Guide,*
> *And run not before Him whatever betide;*
> *In joy or in sorrow, still follow thy Lord,*
> *And, looking to Jesus, still trust in His Word.*

Take time to be holy, be calm in thy soul;
Each thought and each motive beneath His control;
Thus led by His Spirit to fountains of love,
Thou soon shalt be fitted for service above.
"Take Time to Be Holy" (1882)

If you will only take time, you will surely begin to grow!

Growth is a choice. It's never to late to start
The neat thing about all this is you can choose to start growing again at any time—even if you stopped years ago. Look at the Israelites. Isaiah told them over and over again that there was an ever open invitation to come back to God and begin again. In Isaiah 1:18 the Lord invites Israel to agree with his summary of their situation and "argue" it out together. He promises renewal and restoration to a people who could learn a lot about respect from their ox and donkey (see Isa. 1:3). The broken heart of God echoes through Isaiah's words as he tries to convey to Israel his Father heart and his huge concern that his prodigal children return.

It's the very same today. It doesn't matter where you are or how you are or who you are—spiritual dwarf or no; God is waiting, and when you return, you'll say, "I should have come sooner!"

Just as there is no growth without the right attitude, there is no growth of the soul without real continuous action, and that means daily discipline. Discipline is action, responding to the right attitude developed in your time with God. Discipline follows through and does something about growing the soul. What actions can we discipline ourselves to take?

FEED ON WHAT NOURISHES. First and foremost we can watch our diet. Just as my little friend needed to grow physically by eating regularly and nutritiously, so we need to grow spiritually by deciding to have a good diet. Healthy soul food is more important than physical food.

In a certain impoverished area of the world there is a root that is called *naroo*. It tastes good and fills you up. A group of people began to use it in their diet, and because it tasted sweet and other food was scarce, they ate more and more of it and less and less of anything else. In the end, malnutrition and death visited that group of people, and questions began to be asked. Why had these people died? After all, they had had plenty of *naroo* to eat! It was discovered that *naroo* had absolutely no nutritional value. These people were starving to death while being full of *naroo* and feeling satisfied!

Our spiritual diet is very important, too. What we read and how we read and interpret what we read will determine our growth or demise! Some practical ideas about good spiritual food:

- Buy a good evangelical study Bible (get ideas from your local bookstore) and read a portion every day with the help of the commentary and notes already in the text. *Oxford*

- Sign yourself up for a good systematic daily Bible reading plan, e.g., Scripture Union, P.O. Box 6720, Wayne, PA 19087-8720. This plan has Bible notes at all levels and for all ages.

- Join a Bible study group.

- Take a notebook and pencil along with you to church to take notes. This spiritual diet should be uppermost in our mind and always take precedence over our physical diet!

A pastor in Africa who was starving was asked by a relief worker, "I know you and your people are believers and pray the Lord's Prayer every day. How do you handle the verse in the Bible that says, 'Give us this day our daily bread'?"

"Well," replied the pastor (whose soul had grown bigger and bigger as his stomach got smaller and smaller), "I have come to understand that physical food must not be the most important thing!"

Although God in his strange, sovereign purpose may choose to withhold our daily bread, he promises never to withhold our soul food. There is a fullness of being that only his Word and presence can fill. When his Word becomes our most necessary food, we will start to sing songs of joy and satisfaction however many real calories we eat.

So how do we eat this soul food he promises to provide? What is it? Where do we get it? It is food from the prophets like Isaiah. It is food from the patriarchs, the apostles, and teachers of Scripture.

> *The answer now as then, for all of us who would be "growing in our knowing," is to feed the soul and starve the flesh.*

The children of Israel in Babylon probably had only the book of Isaiah to read. The New Testament hadn't been written, and their sacred books were gone, buried in the rubble of Jerusalem. But they had Isaiah! He was available, and what a feast he provided for his people. Yet there is not too much indication that they took advantage of such a priceless opportunity. "Oh," you say, "if I had the book of Isaiah sitting on a shelf in my tent, I'd read it!" Would you? Would I? Just think of the glut of material we have available to us here in the U.S. Do we take advantage of the "prophets"—teachers, Bible commentaries, videos, tapes, fellowship, seminars—right here in our "tent" or the one next to ours? So often Christians seem to have a severe case of spiritual anorexia nervosa. People having this serious physical disorder willfully starve themselves to death in the midst of plenty. If we are going to discipline ourselves to take action and provide spiritual nourishment for ourselves, we must make some decisions not only to regularly listen to our own particular "Isaiah" in church but also to learn how to feed ourselves in between Pastor Isaiah's sermons.

So some of us need to buy a Bible (if we're starting out, the NIV

Study Bible may be a good one to start with) and begin to read it regularly. Three small meals a day is a good idea! After all, we don't starve ourselves all week physically and then eat seven days worth of food on Sunday morning.

STAY CONNECTED TO THE SOURCE OF YOUR GROWTH.

The next action we need to take is to discipline ourselves in prayer. Prayer is our response to what we read in the Bible. Prayer is the place in which we talk to him who has talked to us. It is the place where we "wait upon the Lord" to renew our strength. I don't believe we can grow if we don't pray. Prayer is the Christian's vital breath. For example, as I take time to be holy, I may read in the Bible that I need to grow in my relationships with people in the church. Having read this, I may then think of a brother or sister I'm having trouble with, and I realize I must put things right. I may even find in the text the way I should go about it. There will possibly be some instruction or encouragement there or maybe some promises to claim. Then I'll need to pray about it. Prayer is almost like a digestive process in which we chew over what we've eaten. As we read, mark, and inwardly digest it all in prayer, we have an opportunity to dialogue with God. First, we need to hold ourselves in his presence. This will clarify the mind, nerves, and will.

And after that we will need to exercise our lungs and pass along the message we've received in the prayer room! Tell others about the Lord. Sing the Israelites' songs of his glory, strength, power, mercy, grace, compassion, encouragement, and help. And sing songs of evangelism and invitation to the Babylonians, too.

Have you hung up your harp on the growth tree? Why not take it down. Do you want to be bigger in your spirit? It's entirely up to you!

Growth Marks of Spiritual Progress

How will you know you're growing? Well, how did my little five-year-old friend know he was getting bigger? He could see it!

He could actually monitor his progress. His body got bigger as the days passed by. As he ate his oatmeal and exercised, he could tell the difference as year after year ensued. His mind expanded as he fed it information and intellectual vitamins. His social circle expanded and grew with maturity. His relationships developed along the way, and his soul began to sing a hymn of praise to his God. He only had to look at photographs of himself in the school yearbook to notice the difference.

If we dared to allow the Holy Spirit to show us the photographs he has taken of us for heaven's yearbook, what would the pictures be like? Would we see a bigger body, mind, and schedule—but the same-sized soul?

Evaluate basic areas.

One of the ways I help myself to grow is to evaluate each of these areas—Bible knowledge, prayer, and witnessing—on a regular basis. I measure my progress and make adjustments. For instance, Bible reading: It helps to use a layman's commentary along with a good reference Bible to help me understand the background of the passage. I often make use of a church or seminary library nearby. Sometimes I take a Bible correspondence course or sign up for a theology class in an area in which I'm not familiar. One year I took a hermeneutics class, which helped me learn the rules for interpreting Scripture. There are rules, and we need to learn what they are before we make the Bible say anything we want it to say! If I've lived in the New Testament for a long time, I go to the Old Testament for a period. I also try to have a personal Bible plan when I meet the Lord with no agenda except matters that have to do with him and me! Otherwise, being a teacher of Scripture, I'm forever applying what I read to my next teaching lesson. *Oh, this is just right for Mrs. Smith on Thursday,* I think smugly. In my personal time with God, I give him the chance to address the things he and I need to address in the matter of the growth of *my* soul—not of other people's!

---

*Do we take advantage of the
"prophets"—teachers, Bible commentaries,
videos, tapes, fellowship, seminars—
right under our noses?*

Then there's prayer. I want to be honest in this area, so I pray about my prayer life and ask God to keep me growing in this area, too. I try to evaluate my intercessory prayer. For example, I ask myself, Are the people I am praying for who don't know Christ finding him? I think back to the days I was first converted. I made a lot of friends at college who needed the Lord. I began to pray for them one at a time until they were converted; in six months all of them had made commitments. Not long ago I was thinking about that list and realized I had long since stopped being so specific in my prayer life for my unbelieving friends. In fact, there had been very little growth in that particular area of my prayer life. As I thought about that, I began to put together a new list! I told the Lord, "Grow me up here, Lord. Make me an effective weapon in prayer to do battle for my friends. May everyone on this list find you."

As far as witnessing is concerned, I ask God to help me take initiatives not only in prayer but in friendships. I try to make friends with as many Babylonians as possible. I could easily spend my days among Christians and find myself in an evangelical sub-culture that has isolated me from the real world. I have to work at this. Not long ago we moved into a new house. I began to pray for my new neighbors. "How can I meet them all at once, Lord?" I prayed. We had built a house on a small lake. There were fifteen other homes around the lake.

The first summer in our new environment we discovered an invasive weed spoiling our pretty waterway. Because my husband and I feel responsibility to care for our God-created environment, I called the Department of Natural Resources for help. Now I had not been conscious of trying to grow in the area of friendship evangelism, and if I had not been praying specifically for my new neighbors, I might have missed the idea I believe was generated by God. One man came to me. "Why not pull everyone together and form a loose lake association?" he said. We could meet around a common interest and concern and see where things went from there. I wrote a letter and posted it in everyone's mailbox. My next-door neighbor helped me. They all came. In one evening we had the privilege of hosting the entire lake community in our home. We have since had another get-together and have planned the next one. At once, "Jesus connections" began to announce themselves. All sorts of contacts were made these evenings. These are sweet people, new friends, and now I have another list! Every so often I find I need to take an initiative to reach out to my own home crowd. I certainly make it a matter of prayer and try to watch myself to make sure I'm growing in this area.

Not infrequently a person will come to mind who isn't on my list, and it could well be the Spirit is prompting me to contact him or her and just pray for that person.

We can know we are growing if we discover a new awareness of the Lord and his purposes, a new compassion for the needy, a new concern for the lost, and a new sense of urgency to reach out to others' needs in these present times.

How   We can know we are growing if we find ourselves giving to the point of sacrifice, serving the community, stretching and reaching for spiritual goals, and passing on our faith to our generation—and the next—in ever increasing measure! We can know we are growing when we can't get enough of all of the above.

We can also know we are growing when the fruit of the Spirit blossoms in our life. Take a good look at 1 Corinthians 13:4-6. See how much the fruits of love, patience, kindness, self-control, and unselfishness flourish in your life. Are you more patient this year than last year with that difficult teenager? Are you kind and considerate or touchy with an unbelieving husband? Are you in control of your health and wealth? The areas of health and wealth are great measuring sticks for spiritual growth! Spiritual growth means that a biblical attitude toward our health and wealth will be learned and its principles put into practice. Do I think of my body as "the temple of the Holy Spirit"? Do I abuse it in any way? And do I consider my money my own or count myself a steward of the riches, however few or many, God has entrusted to me? Can God even trust me with resources? That's a question we have to answer alone before the Lord. It took me a lot of growing before I really appreciated I was spending someone else's money every time I wrote a check. It's easy to evaluate my learning curve in this area. I can add up my tithes and offerings at the end of the year and look at the bottom line with the Lord!

Are you, in effect, more like Jesus or less like him than when you first came to faith in Christ? In all these ways you can evaluate your progress, make adjustments, and grow.

I haven't really mentioned church in all of this. Elsewhere I've drawn attention to the need for fellowship and service, but there's one other dimension I would add. Growth can be measured by my participation and growing effectiveness in the local body of believers of which I am a part. Can I look back and measure that? I believe so.

I was really amused by a cartoon depicting an elderly lady sitting in a rocking chair in the church nursery. The caption underneath said, "I only came in here twenty years ago to let Billy go to the bathroom!" If we have fallen into some responsibility in the church because someone fell out of it—or if we are "stuck" feeling like a square peg in a round hole—we need to recognize a lack of growth in that area! Maybe a note to a leader or pastor to talk over such matters would be appropriate.

Do we need to hone our leadership skills, polish our fellowship skills, or learn some fellowship skills? Where and how do we need to grow? It all depends if we are honest and earnest, really earnest, about our own spiritual growth.

LEARNING TO SING AGAIN

S P E N D I N G   T I M E   T O G E T H E R

For couples, families, Bible study groups, Sunday school classes, or for family devotions

1. Read Romans 6–8. How do these chapters relate to spiritual growth? Make lists of things about

THE FLESH (old nature)	THE SPIRIT (new nature)

2. What part do the Bible and prayer play in having victory over the flesh?

3. Share a favorite hymn, passage of Scripture, or wise word that has helped you to grow.

4. What part has the church played in your spiritual life and growth?

5. Pray together about all of the above.

SPENDING TIME ALONE

1. If you want to be "bigger," where do you need to begin with your attitude or actions?

2. Write a paragraph to the Lord. Tell him at what stage of growth you are:

- infant

- youth

- young adult

- middle age

- mature

3. Do you want to be bigger? Which action must you take in order to begin to grow?

- Read the Bible

- Pray

- Share what I'm learning

4. Spend time praying about your answers to the above questions.

5. Pray for someone you know who is suffering from spiritual anorexia nervosa. Who is eating *naroo*?

6. Pray for your "Pastor Isaiah."

CHAPTER FIVE

THE GRIND TREE

Work hard and cheerfully at whatever you do, as though you were working for the Lord rather than for people.

Colossians 3:23, NLT

L/ord of the pots and pans and things,
since I've no time to be
a saint by doing lovely things,
or watching late with thee,
or dreaming in the dawnlight,
or storming heaven's gates . . .
make me a saint by getting meals
and washing up the plates.
Thou who didst love to give men food
in room or by the sea,
accept this service that I do—
I do it unto thee.

This anonymous poem illustrates the apostle Paul's advice to slaves.

> You slaves must always obey your earthly masters, not only trying to please them when they are watching you but all the time; obey them willingly because of your love for the Lord and because you

want to please him. Work hard and cheerfully at all you do, just as though you were working for the Lord and not merely for your masters, remembering that it is the Lord Christ who is going to pay you, giving you your full portion of all he owns. He is the one you are really working for. (Col. 3:22-24, TLB)

He is Lord of the pots and pans and things! He is the one who can take the daily grind and turn it into the daily glory!

Caught in the Daily Grind

You might think you are caught in the daily grind as you "slave" at your housework or your out-of-house job, but just imagine if you were a real slave! The Israelites had been herded like cattle to an area by the river Chebar in Babylon. The idea was to have them dig a deep canal for the king of Babylon so he could sail his ship down it. This might have been fun stuff for the king, but it was not too much fun for the Israelites! It was a backbreaking, heartbreaking job. There were no unions to complain to, no child-labor laws, no pay, no time off, and certainly no vacations. Worst of all there was no relief or end to the misery in sight. Soon the children of Israel were hanging up their harps on the "ground down" tree and descending into bitterness, exhaustion, and depression. It is most disheartening to work a job you hate day after day with seemingly no return, no appreciation, no reward, and no respite! Facing such a dreary routine leaves you emotionally spent even when you've had physical rest.

Elijah's grind

Another kind of daily grind is what we now call burnout. I can't help thinking of the prophet Elijah, who one day lay down under his particular grind tree and prayed that he might die (1 Kings 19:3-4). It wasn't a case of slave labor with him; rather it was a case of running out of steam after three years of sustained pressure. Elijah had experienced being shut up in a confined environment. He suffered a boring routine that must have driven such an activist as he was crazy. For month after month he had been out of a job. What's more, he was in hiding with a price on his head.

It sounds to me as if Elijah was undergoing spiritual fatigue syndrome!

This precarious situation resulted in Elijah living an extremely "daily grind" existence. He had been offered hospitality by a very humble widow woman in a foreign place, but there was little to do, no one stimulating to talk to, and no apparent end to his situation. It must have been most depressing, and although Elijah's daily grind was finally interrupted by some great fireworks on the top of Mount Carmel when he took on the establishment (1 Kings 18:38), he very soon found himself flat on his face under a broom tree, complaining. "'I have had enough Lord,' he said. 'Take my life; I am no better than my ancestors'" (1 Kings 19:4). He was unutterably weary, deeply depressed, and—if not outright suicidal—willing enough to die then and there that he suggested God take his life.

What sort of grind are you in?

Have you been undergoing months and months of grinding pressure? Sometimes we're worn down by the grind but don't realize the grind we're in. Often we don't have a big spiritual problem or a life crisis—but we are also unaware of what's dragging us down.

Take some time to think about and possibly write about what aspects of your life are grinding right now. Put it all out on the table, for you and the Lord Jesus to look at together. Perhaps like Elijah you have not been able to find employment and have been forced to accept charity—a wearing experience!

When my husband and I first went into missions and I

found myself with a traveling husband, all of the daily grinding jobs still needed to be done, and in the absence of Father, Mother did them. Since our salary was meager, we found ourselves often depending on other people's charity. I didn't realize how very wearing that was until one day after I had advertised for a piano for our youth work, I received a phone call from a very wealthy lady I knew. "I saw your advertisement in the paper, Jill," she said. I became very excited—*We're going to get our piano!* I thought. "We have just bought a new Steinway, so I thought you might like our old piano." Years of living off people's secondhand junk suddenly got to me. "No, thank you," I replied quickly—too quickly. "I'd like your new one!" There was a silence, then a cold, curt reply, and I was left clutching the phone, aghast at what I had done. Of course I ended up with no piano at all, which I'm sure served me right. Looking back, I think that the sustained pressure and the dependence on people got to me—the way I'm sure it got to Elijah. It was all just too much, and I suddenly realized I was worn out.

Spiritual Fatigue Syndrome

It sounds to me as if Elijah was undergoing spiritual fatigue syndrome! This is a malady that can be brought on by circumstances both internal and external. We may be able to identify with Elijah's feelings, even if our situation is not as dramatic as his was.

As a wife and grandmother, I can relate to a little of this. There is something extremely wearing about serving others, slaving in the kitchen to produce food that disappears in minutes. And then there are the loads of wash you do one day that need doing all over again a day or two later. Women often accomplish their many tasks without due appreciation, time off, overtime pay—and no end to the situation in sight. This can be depressing in the extreme and can be likened to Elijah's broom-tree blues!

I'm not for a moment comparing the calling of homemaking to

slave labor, but I know more than a few Christian women who do. So how do we aspire to spiritual heights when we're in the physical and spiritual depths brought on by the daily grind?

Get some sleep.

How did Elijah overcome such weariness? First of all, he had a good sleep! Then he had a good meal, and then he had another good sleep (1 Kings 19:5). Even though there was much more than physical burnout going on in Elijah's life, God first gave him a break, cooked him a great breakfast, and encouraged him to have a vacation! If it's possible to do so, that's where those of us who have lost our joy under the grind tree may need to begin. As an Elijah-type person who loves to be doing things, I need to give myself permission to rest and recuperate. To relax is work for me! Sometimes I literally need to take my calendar off the wall and write on it "Have fun 4:30 Thursday," or it doesn't happen.

Take time to listen to God.

After Elijah had rested, he started to listen—really listen—to God. He needed to get away and "stand on the mountain in the presence of the Lord" (1 Kings 19:11). He needed to physically extract himself from his environment and put himself in a situation conducive to hearing the still small voice of God.

This is often one of the last things we do instead of one of the first things. Elijah found a cave and gave himself a chance to wait on the Lord to renew his strength.

I think that often this is the very part of our spiritual upkeep that eludes us. Maybe there is no possibility in your life for such solitude as a "cave." It doesn't sound as if the slaves in Babylon had the luxury of going to a cave, either. No chance of a vacation on a lovely mountain for them.

If we can't physically go to a place of solitude, then we have to travel to that internal mountain of the soul, above and away from the noise and bustle of people. What this usually means is that we learn to listen to God even in the midst of our slaving away.

> *In the daily grind I always find the daily grace I need,*
> *To see in dullness God's sweet way of forcing me to feed.*
> *In pastures green, beside the streams of waters of the*
> *   spirit,*
> *The daily grind I often find brings blessings I don't merit,*
> *Fatigued with dull depressing work and seeming slavery.*
> *If I look up and drink the cup He's offering to me,*
> *However dull or bitter these things He has permitted—*
> *He has power to change my attitude though hardened and*
> *   embittered.*
> *Then soon I'll come to realize this boredom is His gifting.*
> *If I had not been so ground down, how could there be a*
> *   lifting?!*
> —J. B.

Remember Jesus.

I often think of the Lord Jesus and realize he lived in a crowded home probably no larger than our living room. True, he could get away to the desert or the hills or some beautiful garden and did so regularly. But many times he was surrounded by a multitude of needs and had no option but to pray "on the run" just where he was and how he was and whomever he was with.

When the Lord Jesus slaved away for thirty years in his carpenter's shop, he did it as unto the Lord. "I do always those things that please him," he said. We will need to come to terms with our present circumstances in our particular carpenter's shop.

We will need to come to terms with our present circumstances in our particular carpenter's shop.

Whether our daily grind can be interrupted by a trip to the cave or a time to stand on some physical mountain in the presence of the Lord or not—the one thing that can make the difference is the realization that we are not serving people or even companies or institutions; we are serving God. If we do our work with this mind-set, he can energize us as we work and will thus turn our daily grind into something glorious.

Embrace your situation as God's place for you.

One of the things that can grind us down is working well below our gifting and capacity.

Think about Jesus during those Nazareth years. He worked his father's trade day in and day out. He made it his own. He, who had created the mighty trees, pounded nails and sawed that same wood. He needed to provide for a widowed mother (for it is traditionally believed that Joseph died while Jesus was young) and his brothers and sisters. The majority of his short life on earth could be called extremely mundane—what I like to call "Nazareth living." Could he have traveled outside of his podunk town and bettered himself? Of course he could have, but apparently he discerned it to be God's will to spend the majority of his days living out the daily grind in an obscure and despised village. I'm sure you would agree, Jesus was working well below his capacity!

If you're living in Nazareth, one of the secrets of renewed strength is to believe that God has planned for you to live in such a place and have such an occupation—and do it all to the glory of God, do it as unto the Lord. Possibly one of the most important verses in the Bible to do with this is Psalm 139:16. David said, "All the days ordained for me were written in your book before one of them came to be." A sense of God having written down every one of my days with something eternal in mind lifts my attitude from daily grind to daily glory!

This doesn't mean we should not try to better ourselves and

maximize our gifting. But for many of us those opportunities may never happen.

There were no daily days for Mother—only divine ones!

My mother-in-law worked hard all her life. She was an extremely bright and gifted lady. She had wanted to be a nurse, but her father decided she should stay home and housekeep for the family. A woman's place was in the home, he said. During the war, Mother ran the small family grocery business under acute pressure in a Nazareth sort of town in the north of England. She lived every day and accomplished every task as if it were the most important day of her life, even though she never had a chance to develop the many talents she had. Her Lord was truly "the Lord of her pots and pans"!

I remember her cleaning shoes as if Jesus were going to wear them, making beds as if he were coming to stay, and working in her pretty English garden as if her Lord and Savior would be sitting on the little bench by the roses for a brief respite. The English bakery, even on wartime food stamps, was prepared as if Jesus were coming for afternoon tea, and she drove her car as if he were an honored passenger. There were no daily days for Mother—only divine ones! And seeing she believed she was living in "Nazareth" because God had ordained it that way, she felt quite free to draw on his strength for the job. It takes more power to live below our capacity sometimes than when we are stretched beyond it. Over her kitchen sink (well before dishwashers) she hung a plaque with the words "Divine services conducted here three times daily." It was, I can tell you, quite unnerving and did away with any griping while washing up! Needless to say, most times I had the joy and privilege of being around Mother, I would hear her humming or singing a song. One of her favorites was "Forth in Thy Name, O Lord, I Go":

> *Forth in Thy name, O Lord, I go,*
> *My daily labor to pursue,*
> *Thee, only Thee, resolved to know*
> *In all I think, or speak, or do.*
>
> *The task Thy wisdom hath assigned,*
> *O let me cheerfully fulfill;*
> *In all my works Thy presence find,*
> *And prove Thy good and perfect will.*
>
> *Thee may I set at my right hand,*
> *Whose eyes my inmost substance see,*
> *And labor on at Thy command,*
> *And offer all my works to Thee.*
>
> *For Thee delightfully employ*
> *Whate'er Thy bounteous grace hath giv'n;*
> *And run my course with even joy,*
> *And closely walk with Thee to heav'n.*
> —Charles Wesley (1749)

Mother's song of praise was a lesson I've never forgotten. Her testimony to believers and unbelievers alike was powerful. Babylonians are usually amazed at such an attitude. After all, slaves tormented by the daily grind usually have scowls, not smiles, on their faces!

In contrast, I remember another lady who was employed to clean the castle we worked in that served as a youth center. It was a thankless task. Being England where we have only two seasons—winter and the second week of August—three hundred rambunctious European teenagers would run in and out of the castle tracking mucky mud all over the place. One day I came upon this cleaning lady, slaving away with her broom. "Move out of the way," she said curtly. "I need to brush all the dirt out you're tracking in." She began to hum a grim tune (a daily grind composition!) between her teeth. "I'll do my work to the glory of God!" she sang furiously! One look at her grim face made me realize this was not a song of Zion. This woman was an unhappy soul. None of her dreams had been realized, and she felt that none of her gifts were appreciated. How different from my mother-in-law's happy hymn of praise!

Take stock—and take heart!

If you are suffering from spiritual fatigue syndrome, think through the principles we've just discussed.

- What physical things could you do to renew your body, mind, and spirit? Do you need some sleep and healthy food?

- How can you go to a cave of your own and be renewed in the Lord? Is there a place? Or are there a few moments in each day or evening you could dedicate to this waiting to hear from God?

There was a time in my life when I was a young mother chafing at living in Nazareth. All my children were under school age, and my husband's job necessitated his being away many months out of the year. It was really difficult to get involved in any outside ministry. One day I thought about it and realized the Lord was asking me to be content to serve at home first, to put as much energy and creativity into my homemaking as my speech making. Then and only then would he use me outside the home. So I set about the job of mothering with everything I had. There was no Sunday school in the area, so I just began to gather the children around our house into our living room and create one. Actually, it was for our own kids. Soon there were over fifty kids each week. Of course, kids have parents, and so I'd throw in a few parents' days here and there. Some needed to know more about the Lord, so I started an evangelistic Bible study, to which they began to come and bring their friends and family. There were some who were elderly and needed practical help, so the children and I began to help them.

Suddenly I looked around my Nazareth and realized a full-blown ministry was going on—and the heart of it was my own home! Our children all served at their own level. For example, Judy helped me tidy up and clean the living room for Sunday school; David passed out the song sheets; and Pete (age three) took the offering, counted it, and put it in "Jesus' piggy bank" that stood on the dresser. Later in the week when I'd baked the teatime treats, Dave would get some of the Jesus piggy bank money and tuck it into a corner of the bakery box that they all helped pack. Then we'd get into the car and go to one of the grandmas who needed help. Judy would knock on the door, Pete would toddle in with the bakery goods, and David would give the hug or handshake, whichever he thought appropriate. Our Nazareth days rushed by far too quickly for my liking, and I realized not only had I found that my spiritual fatigue had lifted, it seemed that my physical stamina had increased.

Why don't you invite Jesus into your Nazareth and allow him to look around and assess the situation? Then start where you are in the heart of your home and serve the people nearest to you. You will, I believe, find that lots of other people will undoubtedly find a whole new life.

What's Your Compensation?

Another wearing element that can cause many of us to feel like slaves and hang up our harps is the issue of adequate compensation. You expect to be remunerated appropriately for whatever job you are doing. Sometimes however, it's hard to be a stay-at-home mom and feel you have received any or adequate reward for all your labor of love. Certainly you usually don't receive a paycheck for it! Likewise, a lot of jobs require a lot from us but pay very little in terms of wages or benefits. Many people in the workforce today have lost any song of joy they may have had, simply because they are getting so little tangible return.

But think of all the work the talented, educated children of Israel were doing—and would do to the end of their days—without any hope of remuneration! What positions had some of them held in Jerusalem? Had they been leaders, educators, doctors, money lenders, teachers? Certainly some of them had been accustomed to a moderate, if not high, standard of living, back before their days of captivity and servitude. But now they found themselves working for someone else's benefit—someone else whom, as Jews, they abhorred. What an insult to have so much demanded of them with only a whiplash in return. No wonder a loud silence settled over their work camps at the end of the day—unless, that is, like Isaiah and Elijah and Mother Briscoe, they were working for eternal rewards "as unto the Lord."

Not the servant of people, but God's freedman or freedwoman

The thing that makes a huge difference when you're slaving away at the daily grind is to start thinking of yourself, not as the family servant, but as the Lord's freed person.

I am not suggesting that we don't try and better ourselves or take the freeing opportunities that come our way. In fact, Paul encourages that. In the Hebrew tradition, as stated in Old Testament law, the Year of Jubilee was an opportunity for slaves to be emancipated by their owners. Most took advantage of it.

But in the New Testament accounts, when Jubilee no longer applied, the gospel helped slaves who couldn't gain their freedom become willing slaves of the Lord Jesus Christ. Through that commitment they began to do everything they did for their earthly masters "as unto God."

I remember being a young student teacher and finding myself in a situation with a real slave driver of a supervisor—a full-blooded Babylonian! She worked me harder than I had ever worked in my life and got rid of all her own dirty work and the mundane stuff by dumping it on me. She was a fearsome taskmaster. She was also unfair, demanding things of me I found increasingly impossible to give. She reminded me of the Egyptian slave masters who demanded the Israelites make bricks without straw (Exod. 5:10-19).

Then I tried to treat each and every daily day as a challenge instead of a chain.

If I had not just been converted to Christ and become a new creation in him, I would not have put up with this treatment for a minute. But now I believed I had no option; I believed God had led me to choose teaching as a profession for some future calling and that what I did by this particular river of Babylon was all part of God's will involving my training. This preparation of character undoubtedly included my attitude toward this fearsome lady, who was my "master."

Seeing I was now the slave of Christ, I tried to look at each task she gave me as if Christ had asked her to ask me to do it. Even if she demanded the impossible—that is, asked me to make bricks without straw—I would try, for after all, I was the Lord's freedwoman!

The difference was incredible! I cleaned out the hamster and mice cages singing, "All things bright and beautiful, all creatures great and small," focusing on the mice, not the muck! Next I began to pray fervently that my Babylonian taskmaster would become a slave of Jesus like me. Then I tried to treat each and every day as a challenge instead of a chain. It worked! As I sat under my grind tree one day, I looked above my head and found it empty, for my harp was in my hand, and I would not shut up!

How do you get the wind of the Spirit in your wings and become heaven conscious instead of earthbound? You wait on the Lord and submit to him, living as his freedman or woman. Then you will find that "prison bars do not a prison make."

I am always amazed how this mind-set—what I am doing for others I am doing for him—transforms the actual task and lightens the load. There was an incident in our family when four little children under the age of five needed my care for a couple of weeks. I loved my grandchildren to death, but the energy level I needed was beyond me. As I waited on the Lord and served those little children, I drew on his patience when I ran out of mine, his kindness when I was tempted to be short, his peace when I couldn't find the children for a half hour (they were playing hide-and-seek), his self-control when they all pushed the limit at the same time, and his joy when I was mopping up the debris at the end of the day wishing I was in bed! I sat down with my Bible and a cup of tea late each night and said, "Lord, thank you that I have served you today. For you said that as much as I have done it unto one of 'the least of these,' I've done it unto you—and I've done it unto four of these little ones! I feel as fulfilled here at the end of the day as I do standing on a platform in front of thousands of people because *this* has been my assigned, ordained task for you. Thank you for the joy and the privilege." The understanding that I was serving God in these little people enabled me to go beyond the edge of my resources, to run and not be weary and walk and not faint. There is a sense of being the Lord's freedwoman at times like these.

Waiting on the Lord in the midst of the grind

This waiting on the Lord is not a passive exercise conducted in a vacuum. I have absolutely no doubt in my mind that the slaves had no private place where they could go to meditate or study Pastor Isaiah's sermon notes. Their waiting, so often like our waiting, had to be done in the middle of the muddle, in the midst of the mess! Sometimes we must do it under the hot sun, and sometimes we must do it at the bottom of the ditch with the shout of the taskmaster ringing in our ears. We must be in touch with the Master on a moment-by-moment basis while the sweat and toil are at their worst. We must learn to go to the "waiting room"—our internal and eternal refuge—constantly, until the songs of Zion dominate our thinking.

It only takes a second to invite the Lord to listen to the harsh word we have just received. A glance heavenward will help us to tackle yet another pile of dirty soccer laundry or edit and correct boring end-of-term papers. When we practice the presence of God in the daily doings of our life, we shall find ourselves running and not being weary and walking and not fainting.

A Willingness That Marks Us as God's Own

Back to the Year of Jubilee. In this year the slave master was obliged to offer the slave his freedom (Lev. 25:54). If the situation had been a mutually beneficial one (very rare) the slave could say, "I love my master; I will not go out free." At this the master could take his slave to a public place and pierce his ear with an awl, and he would serve him forever (Exod. 21:6).

What a vivid picture this presents. Such a marked man would draw constant attention to the fact of his willing love and service for his master. Notice I said love and service. I knew in my own experience those two elements of my relationship with God must go together. To say, "I love my Master" may sound impressive. To talk long and lovingly about Jesus, to sing praises to him on a Sunday, to write about him and teach about him is commendable. But if I don't marry my verbal expressions of love to service for others, to actions that speak louder than any words—after a while no one will notice what I say. It is in my love labor for him I am seen to belong to my Master, Jesus. In this way I am marked as clearly as a slave with a pierced ear.

I hesitated to say, "I love you, and God does too" and then wave her off on a thirty-mile hike.

Last fall some friends visited us and were helping to landscape our yard. In the middle of the hardest day's work, a young girl came walking up our driveway. We live in the country, and it was obvious that she had walked a number of miles. She had a car, she said, that had broken down, and she needed to get to the bus station—thirty miles away. She was roughly nineteen years of age and reminded me by her dress and language of the European youngsters Stuart and I had worked with years ago. She told me that she had been in a bit of trouble. So I brought her in, and she phoned her father and asked him to come and get her. "He said no," she said in a flat voice, putting the phone down.

"How then will you get home?" I asked.

"He said, 'Walk,'" she responded.

"There's a bus stop near here," I suggested.

"I've no money," she said. I called the bus station but found out the buses didn't run during the day. I relayed this information. As I looked at her crestfallen and worried face, I loved her. She needed Christ. Her fugitive spirit danced away from me, but I started to try and win her confidence.

I would tell her of God's love, I decided. But I hesitated to say, "I love you, and God does, too" and then wave her off on a thirty-mile hike. That would sound a little hollow, don't you think?

My friends from out of town were hauling mulch and digging in bushes, and I knew I needed to stay and help, but I could not say to this girl, "I love my Master" without adding the second part: "I will not go out free." I must serve this one in Jesus' name because I was the Lord's servant. I must put out with no hope of return or reward because I served the Lord Christ. I must be this girl's slave because I was his! So I put her in the car and drove her the thirty miles to a bus depot. Before I left, I picked up one of my books (*There's a Snake in My Garden*, Harold Shaw Publishers, 1996) that tells about my own conversion and the story of the young people Stuart and I served who came to Christ in those far-off days in England.

At last, after drawing her out on that thirty-mile journey, we arrived at the bus depot. We waited for the bus. I smiled at her, gave her some money to get home, and offered her the book. Interrupting her many thanks, I said, "Read this and perhaps you will understand a little about me and about the one I love and serve. Then maybe you'll see why it has been my joy to do this for you."

Then the tears came. Would they have come, I wondered, if I had sat in my pretty house with a kid in trouble and said, "God loves you and has a wonderful plan for your life—start walking"? I think not. Love and love's actions must go together to draw attention to him alone, who is the answer to all our needs.

If a slave by the waters of Babylon could have turned the other cheek, prayed for those who mistreated him, worked as diligently on that canal when the slave driver's back was turned as when he was standing over him; and if he could have helped his fellowmen whether they were Babylonians, Israelites, or foreign slaves from another conquered people—simply and only because he served Jehovah—he would have drawn the attention of all to the one they worshiped in spirit and in truth. On the way they would also have discovered that this attitude of being the Lord's freedman does indeed transform the daily grind into daily glory! Now that's something to sing about. George Matheson gives us words to use to this end in his hymn "Make Me a Captive, Lord":

> *Make me a captive, Lord,*
> *And then I shall be free;*
> *Force me to render up my sword,*
> *And I shall conqueror be;*
> *I sink in life's alarms*

When by myself I stand;
Imprison me within Thine arms,
And strong shall be my hand.

My heart is weak and poor
Until it master find;
It has no spring of action sure—
It varies with the wind;
It cannot freely move
Till Thou hast wrought its chain;
Enslave it with Thy matchless love,
And deathless it shall reign.

My power is faint and low
Till I have learned to serve;
It wants the needed fire to glow,
It wants the breeze to nerve;
It cannot drive the world
Until itself be driv'n;
Its flag can only be unfurled
When Thou shalt breathe from heav'n.

My will is not my own
Till Thou hast made it Thine;
If it would reach the monarch's throne,
It must its crown resign;
It only stands unbent,
Amid the clashing strife,
When on Thy bosom it has leaned,
And found in Thee its life.
—George Matheson (1890)

What marks do you bear as a servant of God?

Are you a marked man or a marked woman or teenager? My husband met with a fifteen-year-old who cares for a disabled child during Sunday morning services. When he asked this young man how he came to do this, he explained that he himself had had cancer, so he really understood and could be patient. "It's so rewarding," he said with a grin. No sense of slavery here; "he loves his Master and will not go out free"!

Perhaps we could look around us and examine the potential for serving others right under our nose. "Who needs my help?" we could ask ourselves. Start with your family, your neighbors, the church family, your workmates. When I was first converted, the girl who led me to Christ suggested I ask people, "How can I help you?" "Whom do I ask?" I inquired. "Everyone you meet," she replied cheerfully. "This way you can begin to serve them and in doing so, serve the Lord." I learned early in my Christian walk that the Lord's service is a very down-to-earth business. It doesn't only have to do with singing in the choir, leading Bible studies, or running committees but involves just being cheerfully helpful!

One of my favorite verses of Scripture is 2 Corinthians 9:7 in which Paul is talking about giving. He says that the Lord loves a cheerful (the word means "hilarious") giver. We are not—he warns—to give grudgingly or of necessity. Remember that some of his teachers were slaves. What a transformation when some of those slaves began to serve their masters—most of them Gentiles—with hilarious joy in the very service they rendered. What a mark that must have made for the Lord and the kingdom. Whether we live in Nazareth, Jerusalem, Corinth, or Babylon, we could aim to do the same.

LEARNING TO SING AGAIN

SPENDING TIME TOGETHER

For couples, families, Bible study groups, Sunday school classes, or for family devotions

1. What aspects of my life could be described as Nazareth living?

2. Can I make changes in my situation that would help me? How would it alter things?

  • What change could I start with?

  • When will I begin?

  • How will I implement it?

3. Read Luke 10:38-46. What aspects of the daily grind were "grinding" on Martha? What was the result of Martha's attitude on her relationship with the Lord? What did Jesus say about it? (Paraphrase in your own words.)

4. What is the Lord saying to me about Martha?

5. What is the Lord saying to me about Mary?

6. Use George Matheson's hymn on pages 105–106 as a prayer. Pray for the Babylonians you serve.

SPENDING TIME ALONE

1. Read 1 Corinthians 7:20-23.

- What shouldn't a slave do?

- What should a slave do?

- How does this apply to my circumstances?

2. Read Colossians 3:22-25. Put in your own words what these verses tell us about a slave's

- attitudes

- actions

- assets

How does this apply to me today?

3. Make a list of things that you need to do today that could come under the heading "Today's Daily Grind."

- Commit yourself in prayer to do them for the Lord.

- Thank God for the privilege of doing these things.

CHAPTER SIX

THE GRATING TREE

When the teachers of the law who were Pharisees saw [Jesus]
eating with the "sinners" and tax collectors, they asked his
disciples: "Why does he eat with tax collectors and 'sinners'?"
Mark 2:16

L et's face it, some of us just don't like Babylonians or Edomites! If we're honest we'll admit it. They grate on us. There's no love lost between us and those folk with whom we have absolutely nothing in common. The idea that they need the Lord does nothing at all to an entrenched attitude deep down inside our spiritual psyche. In fact, if the truth be known, we want to go to heaven, but if we arrived there and found ourselves sitting at the marriage supper of the Lamb alongside one of "those" people, we'd perhaps lose our appetite. It's grating that Jesus told us to love those who grate on us! (He wouldn't even be satisfied with our simply liking them!) When we lose our passion for people simply because they are different from us or irritate us, we lose our joy!

Jonah springs to mind. Jonah was the man God wanted to send to the Ninevites. Perhaps the Ninevites were a few rungs farther down on the food chain than the Babylonians. They were a cruel bunch with little tolerance or respect for human life and dignity. Jonah knew that if he preached "judgment to come" to them, they might repent. That would make them his brothers, and that grated on him. Being a true-blue Jew, he wanted the Assyrians (as the Israelites wanted the Babylonians) wiped off the face of the earth. So he ran away. God, however, had longer legs than he had and circumvented his race to seclusion. He sent a fishy submarine to bring Jonah back to his port of call and duty! Furious—but no doubt fearing another "in depth" experience—Jonah began preaching to the Ninevites. The more he preached, the more they repented, and the more they repented, the more it grated on Jonah. No joy here! In the end, everyone in Nineveh—even the king and queen—repented, which left one very angry and upset prophet sitting alone on a hill under a vine that had mysteriously grown up all in a night to shade him from the fierce sun. When the vine withered, Jonah was furious with it, and God began to deal with the inappropriate anger and frustration in the prophet's heart!

At the root of Jonah's anger was a discontent with the mercy of God demonstrated to people he didn't like.

At the root of Jonah's anger was a discontent with the mercy of God demonstrated to people he didn't like. When it came to his dealings in grace with the Ninevites, God was on his own as far as Jonah was concerned. Prejudice, pride, pique—all raged in Jonah's heart. Yet I like to believe it all changed as God reasoned with his servant and touched his heart, turning prejudice and hatred into love. I like to think this is what happened because it is believed that Jonah wrote the book. It's his testimony.

How do we get along with and love people who are diametrically opposed to all we stand for? We get among them as Jonah did—even if our only motivation is the fear of God and obedience to him—and work with them. Over time, God will work inside us, tuning our heart to sing his praise.

I've come to believe that God will engineer circumstances that throw us into contact with our people prejudices. He will also help us to see these meetings as "God happenstances." We will find ourselves thinking, *This is no accident; it is no coincidence that I find myself rubbing shoulders with people I don't like and who don't like me.* The spiritual remnant among the Israelites learned to say to themselves: "We understand we got into this mess through our own stupidity, and who knows how this ultimately fits into God's universal plan of salvation for us and for his world? But one thing we do know, we have the chance to share our faith with people we would otherwise never have met!"

Facing the People Who Grate on Us

When I began teaching, I found myself handling a classroom full of underprivileged kids from the rough part of the great city of Liverpool. It was a whole different world from my own. I had grown up wealthy and pampered, isolated, and protected from the company of those less fortunate than myself. My life had consisted of living in a "Jerusalem" of classy schools, enjoying vacations abroad, playing in tennis tournaments, and rejoicing in an upper-middle-class social life. My school training was at a teachers college in Cambridge among British elite, where I found Christ. Suddenly the whole of my world turned upside down—or right side up to be exact! After graduation, back in Liverpool at my downtown school, I found myself among a crowd of small, fierce Babylonians! They were rude, rough, foulmouthed—some even smelled—and they grated on me.

They had, I discovered, older brothers and sisters who had grown up to be older and uglier than their small siblings—or half siblings. They grated on me, too! Then I met their parents—and I began to understand why these youngsters behaved as they did! The parents grated on me worst of all! Why had I applied for this particular job at this particular school? Why hadn't I gone after a job among "my own class" in the snooty suburbs?

He had come to look for and bring home the black sheep, not the cute, little, white woolly ones.

The problem was I was now a Christian—a very new one, but a Christian nonetheless. Now I followed Jesus, who had spent his time on earth among people who should have grated on him. Yet he got more frustrated with his own disciples than with the poor, the lepers, the prostitutes, the disadvantaged, those who smelled, and the outcasts. He "came to seek and to save what was lost," he said (Luke 19:10). To look for and bring home the black sheep, not the cute, little, white woolly ones. He also seemed to thoroughly enjoy the company of these people. I couldn't get by it—he loved them! This helped me come to the conclusion that I was in exactly the right place at the right time and for the right divine reason. The joy of this discovery was life changing. My circumstances were no happenstance outside God's plan for my life. This was home!

I began a youth program off church property with a noble band of teenagers, who ventured out onto the streets with me. We rounded up the brothers and sisters of the small Babylonian hordes I was battling with during the daytime school hours. To our amazement they were reachable, teachable, and lovable, and they welcomed our concern. They listened to our story about Jesus and responded to the gospel. It was wonderful. As I spent more and more time among these kids who were so far removed from my own nice little, trite little world, I noticed they had stopped grating on me! I began, wonder of wonders, to love them, and slowly we began to introduce them to the fellowship of the church.

Now we were in for a shock. These gorgeous young Babylonians we had come to know and love and appreciate grated on the people in the church, who had no intention of knowing, loving, and appreciating them! This should not have been such a surprise! How could we have so soon forgotten our own reactions to them? But we had.

The reasons for the people's prejudices seemed so silly and petty (as silly and petty as mine had been in the near past!). There were problems with the old-timers, who wanted the kids to smarten up for church, get their long hair cut, and dress appropriately. Then I was informed that the parents in the church didn't want their kids contaminated by the new influx of young life. I found out it's one thing to let God change your heart for the Babylonians; it's another altogether to persuade others to change theirs!

It was then I began to notice that these prejudiced people in the church began to grate on me because our kids grated on them! I became prejudiced against them and their prejudices! I was angry, disappointed, and judgmental of their attitudes—and guess what happened—I lost my joy. Little wonder! Just because God had given me a passion for this particular group didn't mean he had to give others the same passion for the same group. I needed to stop and contemplate the time it had taken me to come to this point. I was unwilling to allow the time for those not yet convinced to be convinced.

It was then I began to notice that these prejudiced people in the church began to grate on me because our kids grated on them!

I appealed to a wonderful deacon in our church to help us with the growing mob of street kids coming to our meetings. He came along with a little trepidation but soon jumped into the fray (even though the music grated on him), losing his heart, as we had, to these wonderful youngsters. He became our advocate and go-between with the church. It was this man who encouraged us to concentrate on helping the new life of Christ fill up these young-sters' lives and have the "oldies" come around. "Look at the oak trees, Jill," he said to me one day. "When winter comes, there's still a lot of old leaves hanging all over the trees. But as spring comes and the new sap fills the trees, the old leaves drop off! Concentrate on making sure the new life of Christ is filling up the trees, and these outside accoutrements will fall away.

"All the outward things—dress, hairstyle, ornaments—that festooned these young people's bodies are like old, withered oak leaves in winter. They are part of their old life. If only we can fo-cus on the new life of Christ in them, we will not have to waste all our energy climbing every tree and plucking off all these leaves one by one!" We thanked him for his wise counsel and set out to concentrate on discipling our new believers. As we learned leadership, our friend and mentor was to be proved right. Over time we—old and young, high class and low class, black and white, male and female—ceased to grate on each other and graced each other instead. Love was born.

All our lifestyles, theirs and ours, changed slowly but surely as we grew together. Prejudice is a killing thing and can be found as much inside the church as outside. When things are wrong among fellow believers, joy dies. Trouble and misunderstandings inside the church can do it as easily and thoroughly as trouble with peo-ple outside the church.

Disappointment Can Be Grating

Did Isaiah ever fall out with Amos or other contemporary proph-ets? Did Jeremiah clash with the high priest and the hierarchy of his temple? Oh yes! When other believers or leaders grate on our nerves (and it happens all the time), everyone loses. We not only lose our passion for the lost—but the joy of that passion.

Sometimes we step back into old patterns. Our converts can

blow it, and we suddenly discover that they are grating on us all over again! Dealing with disappointment, especially with young people, can be the most sapping thing imaginable. Isaiah experienced this when Uzziah, a young relative he had nurtured, loved, and influenced, made an incredible mess of his life.

After Uzziah became powerful, his pride led to his downfall.

Uzziah was sixteen years of age when he began to reign in Judah. His father, Amaziah, was a good king as was his father before him, and so Uzziah had a great start. The chronicler divides young Uzziah's reign into two parts. He tells us the good news first and then the bad. At first, blessings and prosperity flowed from Uzziah's obedience. He had everything going for him. He had had the influence and example of a godly father and the prophet Zechariah to disciple him (2 Chron. 26:5). The Bible tells us: "As long as he [Uzziah] sought the Lord, God gave him success." Now there's a statement! He went to war against the Philistines and extended Judah's boundaries. Again, this was not done in his own power but as he waited on the Lord to help him (vv. 6-7). The young man's fame spread as far as the border of Egypt "because he had become very powerful" (v. 8). He restored the vineyards and fertile lands, for he loved the soil (v. 10). He built up a well-trained army and recruited 2,600 leaders under whom were 307,500 fighting men. Then the story continues with these sad words: "His fame spread far and wide, for he was greatly helped *until* he became powerful" (v. 15, emphasis added).

After he became powerful, he began to unwind. Someone has said, "Power corrupts; absolute power corrupts absolutely," and perhaps this was true of Uzziah. The Bible says that, despite his grand start and the influence of both Zechariah and Isaiah in his life, Uzziah's pride led to his downfall after he became powerful.

Ah, there it is. Pride! Pride and prejudice! He began to get ideas of how he wanted to worship in the temple. He negated the strict rules and regulations set up in the Law and, ignoring the frantic protests of the high priest and his fellows, attempted to burn incense on the altar in the temple.

As a result, Uzziah was struck with leprosy as a judgment of the Lord and thereafter lived in a separate house in a state of quarantine till the day of his death.

There is nothing that gets to you more than pouring your life into a kid and then having him or her blow it big time! It was, however, in such a time of disappointment in the year that King Uzziah died that Isaiah saw the Lord sitting on a throne high and lifted up—above the situation. Isaiah saw God absolutely sovereign, absolutely almighty, and absolutely in control. Isaiah waited on the Lord at a point in his life when he was in personal pain and in political jeopardy. He knew where to turn for help! Isaiah was getting nowhere with the people of God or their leaders, and now his protégé in whom he had invested so many of his hopes and dreams lay dead with leprosy. That must have grated on his spiritual nerves! However, Isaiah went to the waiting room to renew his spiritual strength, saw the Lord, and affirmed his faith in the fact that God was indeed sovereign. It was then he saw himself in contrast. "There but for the grace of God go I," he said in effect. "Woe to me! . . . I am ruined! For I am a man of unclean lips, and I live among a people of unclean lips, and my eyes have seen the King, the Lord Almighty" (Isa. 6:5). When the brothers were grating on him, it helped the prophet to realize that he was probably grating on them, too. Isaiah realized he was just as much of a sinner as his congregation!

However, we are only responsible for our reaction and response, not other people's, and Isaiah knew he couldn't please the Lord if he wasn't willing to be faithful when others weren't, be stable when others were wobbly, and stand firm when others fell. He needed to keep on keeping on. Isaiah determined to go on with God in spite of Uzziah's fall and death. "Here am I. Send me," he offered in response to the Lord's query, "Whom shall I send? And who will go for us?" So God did send Isaiah. To whom? Back to the very people who had been grating on him for six long chapters of his life!

There is no end to the people in the church of Jesus Christ who will grate on us before we arrive home in heaven! The people in the pew and the people in the pulpit and the people in the periphery of a church family will take their turn rubbing us the wrong way. But the thing we need to come to terms with is that the body of believers is "family," whether we like it or not. Just like our physical family, some of its members will be dear to us, and some will drive us crazy. Some will be close, and some will be distant. Some of us will do well together, and some, despite our best efforts, will repulse our attempts to reach out to them. Then we need to try and do what we need to do and leave the rest to God.

Criticism Grates

I haven't a doubt in my mind that Isaiah was often criticized and ostracized by the leaders of Israel, and it grated on him as much as he grated on them! In fact, he refers to the fact in his book. This is a prime place to lose our joy. We can all hang up our harps because we are unfairly criticized. Leadership is a lonely place to be!

Paul the apostle knew all about being criticized unfairly. Paul grated on not a few of the leaders of the early church. In 1 Corinthians 4:3-4 he tells us how he coped. He said, "I care very little if I am judged by you or by any human court; indeed, I do not even judge myself." He didn't say he didn't care if he or his ministry was grating on people. He said he cared enough to take the matter to the "Lord who judges me." In other words, he waited on the Lord about it.

Our service must be "as unto the Lord" and not "as unto men."

We must learn first and foremost to get our help and encouragement from God alone. Then we must ask God what, if anything, we
should own of the criticism we are receiving. If we can be transparent with the Lord, who, incidentally, knows better than we do, and
be willing to expose our own motivations—our hurt, pique, anger,
irritation—and let him give us input, we will then be able to be
open to discern any directive he gives us. We will also find rest for
our irritated spirits! We will discover an ability to leave the final
vindication of ourselves with him.

> *Here we were all grating on each other instead of
> being grateful for each other!*

All of us like to be liked. But let's face it: If our ministry is going
to be effective, we will end up being thoroughly disliked by someone or other, either inside or outside of the church family! We will
find we can't win. So we will need to strive to be God pleasers and
not people pleasers!

When Stuart and I first moved from England to our church in
the U.S.A., a neighbor invited me to meet her friends and start an
evangelistic Bible study. I was delighted to comply, and after a few
months most of the ladies had come to know the Lord. The group
grew, but since most of the women were from other churches, my
husband suggested we keep the group in a neutral venue lest we be
judged to be "sheep stealing." The whole situation began to grate
on the people in our own church as well as on people from the
other churches; we were accused of sheep stealing anyway! The
fact that my motivations were misunderstood grated on me. My
husband did not appreciate our own church's reaction to his
wife—and, yes, it grated! So here we were all grating on each other
instead of being grateful for each other! That can happen as
quickly as anything in the church family because the devil is there

to stir the pot whenever he sees his chance. We became, quite frankly, weary of it. I had started this grand evangelistic adventure, "flying" spiritually. As the grumbling became audible, it forced me to a running pace, and at the end I was plodding along weary of being weary!

Well, there was one obvious place to go—the waiting room. And there was only one obvious person who could help us—God! Fortunately, enough of us caught up in this situation did just that. The Lord worked in enough of our hearts to resolve the differences, have some honest confrontations, and put things on a good footing. Sometimes in church work you just feel as though you'd like to wrap your harp around the neck of a fellow Israelite instead of composing a song!

Of course, if you're going to try to hold people accountable and responsible to work out their differences, you run the risk of a lot more than merely grating on their nerves. Jeremiah found himself up to his armpits in mud in a deep cistern! How had he merited such torture? For telling the leaders of Israel the truth! So differences aren't always resolved.

The Gospel Will Grate

Church leaders have been martyred and exiled down through the ages. They have been hounded, hunted, and killed for their testimony—for simply telling it like it is. And they have found themselves victims not only of friendly fire but of unfriendly fire! They say there have been more martyrs in the last part of this century than in all of the centuries since Christ. We need to come to grips with the fact that there will be repercussions if we keep the faith, one way or another. If we insist on telling our story of the transforming power of Christ and explaining the gospel outside of our faith circle, we will lose friends over matters of our faith and practice, and we might well gain enemies!

When I came to know Christ as a young student in Cambridge, I faced the prospect of going home at the end of the semester and telling my friends what had happened to me. I knew what their response would be—the same reaction I would have had if one of them had gone away to college and come back converted. In our group, pious religious people had always grated on all of our nerves. We had ridiculed a girl at school who had gone to some religious camp and come home "born again," something that sounded weird to all of us. So I knew what sort of treatment lay ahead of me! I bought some invitation cards and posted them to my six closest friends before I could get cold feet. I invited them to come to my house on Saturday night so I could share some very exciting news with them. I decided to kill six birds with one stone and not mess around. They all arrived with neatly wrapped gifts in their hands—and to my dismay I realized that they had surmised I had gotten engaged! *Oh boy,* I thought, *this is going to be more of a shock than I planned!*

"Well," asked my best friend expectantly, "who's the lucky man?"

"You didn't let the grass grow under your feet," another of the girls murmured admiringly.

"When's the wedding?" a third friend inquired.

"Hey," I interrupted. "This is probably going to grate on you pretty badly, but . . . it isn't a man. Well, what I mean is—I did fall in love—well, not really in love as 'in love'. . . but . . . I've come to know and love Jesus Christ!" There was a shocked silence as my girlfriends stood around me, their presents clutched in their hands, their eyes as big as saucers, and their jaws sagging!

"What?" they echoed, almost in unison.

Stumbling and bumbling, I tried to tell them the little I knew in the best way I could. I was superconscious that they were getting more and more uncomfortable, then upset, then—yes, definitely reactive. I could see that my words were greatly grating.

Soon after, they left. They simply couldn't take it, and that night I lost most of my lifetime friends. One of them actually turned very hostile. They couldn't accept my story. Only one of them stuck by me and eventually came to know the Lord—whereupon she threw a party to tell the rest of her group what had happened to her and found herself ostracized like I had been. Knowing Jesus and making him known has a heavy price attached to it—but a price infinitely worth paying.

Personalities Can Grate

Personality conflicts can be the devil's gateway into a church fellowship. There were two women in the church at Philippi who grated on each other. One was called Euodias and the other Syntyche (my husband renamed them Odious and Soon-touchy!). These women were apparently leaders in the church.

But they had gotten across each other in a big way. Church splits have started from such small beginnings, and Paul, realizing the seriousness of the situation, wrote and pleaded with them to stop their squabbling. I have often wanted to know what it was they were at odds about. Perhaps it was as unimportant a matter as the color of the new church carpet or maybe a difference in ministry philosophy—or even tastes in music! Anyway you can be sure the noises that were emanating from these two ladies' harps were discordant and jarring, and the Lord needed to play some notes of reconciliation on their heartstrings. Paul then appealed to a man in the congregation to step in and try to mediate the problem. He calls him a true yokefellow. That sounds like a very appropriate title for a man about to get between two warring women! He was risking getting his "yoke" thoroughly scrambled! We never do find out if the man was able to help them to forgive each other and work together in harmony, but I like to believe he did and that the work of the wonderful church in Philippi was not hindered by personal conflicts. I have learned to offer myself as a mediator when problems arise. It's usually the last thing I want to do, frankly. I don't need it, as it so often puts me in a no-win situation, but sometimes even if things don't work out, I have the satisfaction of knowing I've tried. I happen to believe we need lots more true yokefellows around church and mission today. Peace in the end doesn't just happen. Peace needs to be made, and peacemakers need to initiate the moves toward reconciliation.

How can this happen?

1. Pray. Ask the Lord if he is asking you to be a true yokefellow.

2. Read the Scripture for confirmation and direction. Look for principles to apply, promises to claim, and practical ideas that may work in this particular situation.

3. Keep a record of what you find. Sometimes what you find can be used in the mediation meeting.

4. Share the dilemma with a trusted friend, and ask for prayer.

5. Pick up the phone, or make contact another way with both parties. A personal handwritten note is better than the computer screen or fax.

6. Offer to mediate.

7. Suggest a time and place if you receive an affirmative response.

8. Call and remind them of the appointment the day before.

9. Enlist some prayer support for all involved over the allotted time of the meeting.

10. Do it!

11. Leave the time with the parties with an offer for a next step. Nail down then and there when to meet again if necessary. Assure both parties of your neutrality and confidentiality and concern. Make sure you open or close with prayer.

12. Spend more time listening than talking.

13. Follow up to consolidate gains.

14. Pray, pray, and pray!

15. Thank God in advance for what he is going to do.

16. Start a training course for other peacemakers!

Are You under the Grating Tree?

What is grating on you just now? Is it a situation or a relationship? Is it something that has caused you to lose your joy? One thing is certain, when we don't attend to sin in our life or jarring relations with people, we will find no inner rest. If we are jarring to others, we need to check to see if it is purely and simply because of Jesus in our life. If it is, we should commit ourselves again to him, who knows our innermost thoughts and motivations, and leave it in his capable hands.

Knowing Jesus and making him known has a heavy price attached to it—but a price infinitely worth paying.

Try to change your focus at this point. Stop looking and listening to others and "turn your eyes upon Jesus." I have found a good way not to hang up my harp on this particular tree is to count my blessings, starting with material ones, then relational ones, then spiritual ones. When you are spiritually battered, it's hard to think of spiritual blessings, but it's easy to think of basic needs that are being met, such as a roof over your head or food in your stomach or clothes on your back. It helps to remember relationships that are intact in your life and praise the Lord for them. Somehow that puts the ones under siege in perspective. Once you're in a "thanking mode," it's easier to begin counting your spiritual blessings. Start with the great blessings of your salvation: forgiveness and peace with God. Thank him for the reality of the hope of heaven and the company of the Holy Spirit. Praise him for the Bible, prayer, and church. It's not all bad—it just looks it at this moment perhaps. A good counting session really helps the joy! Soon you'll find yourself praising him for the sun, moon, and stars, and the whole world, physical and spiritual. As we practice praise, everything will look different.

How to Sing under the Grating Tree

The best way I know to handle a grating problem is to go and do something that pleases the Lord. Perhaps you have tried everything you know how to do to reconcile with someone grating on your nerves, and nothing has worked. Try to leave it with the Lord and involve yourself in some service project for him. Feel his pleasure, and you won't worry too much about anyone else's displeasure!

When I was watching the film *Chariots of Fire,* Eric Liddell was talking about the joy he found in running. "God made me fast," he said, "and when I run I feel his pleasure." I love that phrase "feel his pleasure." He affirms us on the inside, plucking our heartstrings and reminding us, whatever our shortcomings, that he loves us. Knowing we are loved is joy itself.

Much of our frustration is caused by "stuffing" our feelings and not talking about them with the Lord or someone else close to us. My daughter has a two-year-old who has learned to say to his brothers, "You're bugging me" when they are. He feels a lot better when it's out in the open. So will we. It's hard to admit, confront, or engage in dialogue when we're "bugged," but it does no good to pretend it isn't happening. Start on your knees in the waiting room, and after you've vented your feelings, be quiet and listen. Ask the Lord to bring a Scripture to mind, to give you a thought or a good idea. Stay still long enough to have some positive attitude restored. God is so wonderful! No matter how much we bug him, he graciously and patiently suffers our silliness and reminds us he is still our friend. There is such joy in that.

LEARNING TO SING AGAIN

SPENDING TIME TOGETHER
For couples, families, Bible study groups, Sunday school classes, or for family devotions

1. Read Numbers 11. Moses was grating on the Israelites, and the Israelites were grating on Moses.

- How did Moses react? Can you identify?

- How did God respond to Moses? to the Israelites?

- What do you learn about prayer in relation to this incident?

2. Share a personal story (keep it short) of how God resolved a difficult personality conflict for you and one lesson you learned through it.

3. Pray about any ongoing problems

- in your personal life

- at work

- at church

SPENDING TIME ALONE
1. Spend a little time thinking about the things that are grating on you at the moment. Who or what is rubbing you the wrong way? Talk about the situation with the Lord. Ask the Lord if you can do something about it. Decide when. Decide how.

2. Read the Scriptures for fifteen minutes looking for a principle, command, or warning to apply to the situation.

3. Pray for people within the body of believers who are at loggerheads with each other.

CHAPTER SEVEN

THE GLOOM TREE

So my counsel is: Don't worry about things—food, drink, and clothes. For you already have life and a body—and they are far more important than what to eat and wear.

Matthew 6:25, TLB

I've always been a worrier. When I was small, I worried that I'd never grow up to be big. When I was big and realized I had grown up, I worried that I'd never get married. When I was on the way to a wedding, I worried that I'd never experience my own wedding or that I'd be in a car wreck and never make it. Once I was married I began to worry that I'd never have children. After I had three healthy kids, I stepped up my worry machine to third gear. I worried that our toddlers would fall into the washing machine and drown! When they were small, I worried that they'd never grow up to be big; then I worried they'd never get married. On the way to their weddings I worried we'd have a crash and we'd never arrive—and so on and so on! Now we have nine grandchildren, and you can imagine how much I have to worry about!

If there is one place you can hang up your joy quicker than any other, it's on the worry willow—or the gloom tree. Worry can be a chronic spiritual malady that wipes even the hint of a smile off the face of your soul! You can worry about anything and everything. Worriers are really worried when there's nothing to worry about!

And then if they are believers, worriers are genuinely worried about being worried because they know deep down that, being a follower of him who said, "Do not worry" (Matt. 6:25), means they shouldn't be worrying at all!

> **You can trace the root cause of many bodily ills to the curse of chronic worry.**

Worry takes a terrible toll on body, soul, and spirit. You can trace the root cause of many bodily ills to the curse of chronic worry. Heart trouble, ulcers, headaches, and backaches, to name a few. Worry is the sister of mental turmoil, depression, even suicidal notions. The source of all this anxiety, of course, is Satan. He knows that if he can get you all tied up with worry, you won't be able to reach out to Jesus in trust and dependence—which will in the end chase worry out the door.

Waiting on the Lord is the antidote to worry. You can't wait and worry at the same time. It's impossible; try it! The writer of Proverbs reminds us: "A heart at peace gives life to the body" (Prov. 14:30). When you truly trust him, peace comes, keeping not only your body strong but also your very soul.

Worry Then and Now

The Israelites were worried. "Oh, Jerusalem," they moaned. "Jerusalem was our highest joy." They worried about what had happened to Jerusalem. They worried that they might never see Jerusalem again. They worried about the few survivors they had been forced to leave behind. How were they managing? they wondered anxiously. Were they still alive? Were they starving or sick, and if they were starving or sick, were they being mistreated? They worried about their children, who had been separated out and taken to the capital of Babylon to be slaves away from the mass of prisoners in their area. Had the boys been made eunuchs? Had the girls become sex slaves to their masters? Whose husbands and wives had they become? And what about their faith? Slaves were required to take on the beliefs of their owners. Had the brightest and best of their youth recanted and embraced false gods? The Israelites had plenty to worry about. They must have longed to know how to escape the treadmill of worry and find an inner river of peace and tranquillity.

"Wait on the Lord," Isaiah had said. He had already written a great sermon on the text: "You [God] will keep in perfect peace him whose mind is steadfast, because he trusts in you. Trust in the Lord forever, for the Lord, the Lord, is the Rock eternal" (Isa. 26:3-4).

Today people worry about the same sorts of things that the Israelites worried about years ago. What's happening back home? they ask themselves. How are our parents faring? Thousands of refugees in Africa and other nations in trouble worry about their sons and daughters lost in the mass immigrations caused by war and genocide. Christian parents in more secure environments in the Western world worry as their kids go off to secular universities. They drop them off at coed dorms, where access to sex and drugs and dangerous religious philosophies vie for the minds and souls of their Christian children. Will they stand firm? Will they believe anymore? Will they bring a live-in boy- or girlfriend back for the holidays? And if so, what will they do about it? Will their children reject the faith in which they were nurtured? Christian parents let their minds run riot, thereby fixing them on the things that might be, rather than on the one thing that is—namely, the God who is our eternal Rock, the only safe refuge!

It Starts with the Mind

When our mind is stayed on him, it can't be stayed on worrying. It's a good idea to put your head on a pillow of Scripture before you go to sleep at night and in the morning ask God to give you your waking thought. Both exercises have helped me greatly as I have battled the worry war throughout the years. Keeping a devotional by your bedside or reading a Scripture book like *Daily Light*, which collects a few Scriptures under a given theme, just before you close your eyes helps focus your attention where it should be. Likewise disciplining yourself to open your eyes and let your first thought be to let him give you your first thought helps greatly. Then you are also better equipped to help others.

> *Sometime during the day, my husband and I have made it a habit to ask each other, "What has been your best thought today?"*

Sometime during the day, my husband and I will ask each other, "What has been your best thought today?" This helpful little question reminds us that, having started with our mind "fixed on him," we need to steadfastly continue in the same mode! "Great peace have they who love thy law," the psalmist reminds us. And I can tell you that memorizing or shouting a triumphant verse of Scripture at a worry monster sends it scurrying away into the darkness, where it belongs.

The Things We Worry About

We worry that God will not keep his promises.

Some of our worries reveal that we doubt God's ability and willingness to remain God. Worry often discounts the greatness and forgiveness of God. The Israelites were seriously worried that God had forsaken them because they had forsaken him. Would God forgive and restore them and Jerusalem? Isaiah's writings brim over with promises of forgiveness and restoration for them. Prophecies abounded about a godly group among the Israelites who—like himself and his brother prophets down through the ages—would stay faithful to Jehovah and eventually realize redemption and be part of the fulfillment of God's ultimate plan. Yet persistent worry that they had blown it—big time—killed the Jews' joy and filled their minds so they couldn't remember the gracious promises of God.

If we've gotten away from the Lord and lived as if we didn't even know him and then find ourselves in a mess as a result of our own stupid choices, it's easy to worry that there's not enough forgiveness left in God's heart for us! Yet now is the day of salvation and restoration. God is more than willing to restore the joy of our salvation. Worry over the past can keep us from dealing with today and coping with tomorrow.

We worry about things that haven't happened yet.

Worry over the future can be an ongoing killjoy. Somehow we feel that if we worry hard enough, the very energy we put into worrying will stop the boogeyman from getting our children, stop our marriages from falling apart, or stop terrible diseases from destroying us or our loved ones. Reality tells us that some of these things *will* happen. However, when they do, Isaiah reminds us, God will be sufficient. Only a small percentage of bad things will happen, which means most of our worrying is needless. Worry about the future empties today of its strength and leaves us limp and lifeless to face the measure of trouble that may or may not come to us in the future.

We worry about the less important things.

Jesus addressed the subject of obsessive worry when he was on earth. He told us that being anxious (the word he used was one that means the "worry that obsesses") was something that characterized the Gentiles or unbelievers. They worried about food, money, and clothes. They worried about their height, weight, and looks. Jesus did not say these were unimportant things, but he did say they were less important than the most important things. The most important things, he said, were spiritual things, not outward or material ones. The kingdom of God is more important than the empires of men, and living right is more important than being popular, wealthy, or successful. In fact, if we could all start worrying about the right sorts of things—like being Christlike, understanding Scripture, ministering to others, discovering our gifts and place in the church, and winning our world for Jesus—we'd find our worries turned into something valid and useful.

The Other Side of Worry

There are some good things about worry. First of all, worry gives us a chance to trust the Lord and turn our attention to the things that really matter. When I'm worried, it makes me pray and read my Bible more, and that's all good! So anxiety chases us back to God and gives us a chance to turn our worries into prayer. Second, a worrying situation is a good heart check. It makes me ask myself how my spiritual health is. What is my heart focus? Just who is at the center of my life? Around what does my universe revolve?

I love Eugene Peterson's paraphrase of Philippians 4:6 in *The Message:* "Don't fret or worry. Instead of worrying, pray. Let petitions and praises shape your worries into prayers, letting God know your concerns. Before you know it, a sense of God's wholeness and of everything coming together for good will come and settle you down. It's wonderful what happens when Christ displaces worry at the center of your life." But for Christ to displace worry at the center of my life, I need to turn first to him when trouble starts.

Where do I fly to when I am alerted to some gloomy thing threatening me or someone I love? The church, the pastor, my best friend, my children, husband, wife, or God? Whose arms do I fly to first? The answer to that question will in all probability tell me—and those watching me—just who is at the center of my life!

138

> **Worry gives us a chance to trust the Lord and turn our attention to the things that really matter.**

There was a little girl on a train, journeying down England. The passengers were entertained by the friendly youngster, who seemed quite at home with all the passengers in the car. In fact, people began to wonder just who her mother and father were as she seemed at home with everyone. Then the train gave a shrill whistle and entered a long, dark tunnel, and the little girl suddenly became anxious. She ran down the aisle and threw herself into the arms of a young man at the rear of the car. People smiled. Now there was no doubt as to whom the child belonged! She was seen to be happy and safe in her father's arms. Her joy was evident and overflowing. She was still in the tunnel—still in the dark—nothing had changed outside her life, but all was changed inside her life.

There are good things about the situations that make us anxious as we enter the tunnels of trouble along life's track. We are forced to fly into our Father's arms and thereby prove to ourselves, as well as to those around, just who it is we belong to, whom we love, and who it is who gives us joy on the journey—even while we are still in the darkest of tunnels.

We must never underestimate the message God wants to send to a world of worriers who are watching us, either. He wants to show those worriers by our attitude and actions that even when we have a good cause to worry, God can handle it and us! He can take the bad worry and turn it into something useful!

Secure in the Father's Arms

I well remember sitting by a roaring fire on a Sunday during the war years (the Second World War, in case you are wondering). Our family had fled the bombs that rained down on us one night, chasing us hundreds of miles away to the beautiful English Lake District—Wordsworth's country. This was an area of Britain that kept the poets in business, and "seasons of mist and mellow fruitfulness" became part of my heritage.

But that particular day was different. The mists were gone, and a storm had broken over our heads. The rain slashed against the windowpane like giant tears, and the thunder grumbled away as if it were angry it had had to hang around all day. I didn't like storms much. After all, I was young—barely six years of age. I was old enough, however, to understand that there was a bigger storm raging than the one beating against our windowpane. There was a battle going on involving everyone in the whole world. But at that moment it all seemed very far away.

The fire was warm, and my father was sitting in his big chair, relaxed and reading the paper. I could see his face. Suddenly, as if he was aware I needed a little bit of reassurance, he put down his paper and smiled at me. "Come here, little girl," he said in his soft, quiet but commanding voice. Then I was safe in his arms, lying against his shoulder and feeling the beat of his heart! Now, whatever the weather, I could watch the rain and listen to the thunder all day. This was a grand place to be! Why, my father was bigger than any old storm that beat against my window!

I have thought about that incident many times since. When the storms of sorrow swamped me at my mother's funeral, I sought the reassurance of my heavenly Father's presence. When the winds of worry whipped my confidence away as I faced gangs of wild young people in street evangelism, I glanced up to see my Father's face. When floods of fear have risen in my spirit as I waited in a hospital for the results of frightening tests, I have heard my heavenly Father say, "Come here, little girl," and I have climbed into his arms, leaned against his shoulder, and murmured, "This is a grand place to be!"

As I rest in that safe place, believing my Father is bigger than any old storm that beats against the windowpane of my life, I can watch the rain and listen to the thunder and know it's all right. For here I can hear the beat of my Father's heart!

> *Jesus, Lover of my soul,*
> *Let me to Thy bosom fly,*
> *While the nearer waters roll,*
> *While the tempest still is high;*
> *Hide me, O my Saviour, hide,*
> *Till the storm of life is past;*
> *Safe into the haven guide;*
> *O receive my soul at last!*
> "Jesus, Lover of My Soul," Charles Wesley (1738)

As an adult, I have had to learn to fly into my Father's waiting arms just like I did as a child. I have struggled for years in this area, but God has given me release and victory step-by-step. As people have watched me (since I am a public person most of my worrying has had to be done in full view), they have been made to think as they have seen me struggle with this perpetual uneasiness, this chronic, low-grade spiritual headache and negative dread of the future. They have observed that I have been greatly helped by transforming my worries into prayers and trust—and miracle of miracles—joy! Truly I and some of the watchers now understand a little bit better what the peace that passes all understanding really means.

This joyful experience is the birthright of the people of God. This full salvation brings our harps back into our hands in a hurry once we start to trust instead of worry. F. Bottome says it well in a verse in his hymn "Full Salvation."

> *Care and doubting, gloom and sorrow*
> *Fear and shame are mine no more;*
> *Faith knows naught of dark tomorrow,*
> *For my Savior goes before:*

Heartstrings

Full Salvation!
Full and free forevermore.
—F. Bottome, *The Keswick Hymnbook* (p. 61)

We Can Stop Fearing Worry

So as we learn to turn destructive worry to constructive ends, we stop fearing worry! Why, we can even begin to value worrying times, knowing we'll end up with new songs to sing to the Babylonians and new lessons to pass along to our fellow Israelites. It takes a mature person to be glad for the worry if the lessons one learns can help someone else, but I am inching toward being able to be a little bit glad when that happens.

For example, a major tunnel came into sight in my life recently. As darkness fell and anxiety rose in my heart, I flew into my Father's arms. I then became uncomfortably aware this tunnel of trouble was populated with others suffering pain similar to mine. We were all on the same train traveling along the same track! As it happened, I was in the middle of a teaching series from the book of Joshua. As I prepared those messages for others, I discovered God had prepared them first for me! Every message I put together went home to my heart before I ever delivered it from a podium. One day I gave a message on Joshua entitled "Winning the Worry War." I had related to every truth I had discovered as I researched and prepared that particular passage of Scripture.

Here was Joshua commanded by God to march round and round Jericho. I realized that his Jericho represented my Jericho—this impenetrable symbol of the trouble that towered over my life. I woke every morning finding myself like Joshua, walking round and round, round and round my particular Jericho! I couldn't stop my mind marching! At the end of the day I was exhausted, and nothing had gotten done. I had mechanically gone through the motions of business, but I wasn't really "there." It was as if I were on another planet; I was too busy going round and

142

round and round! Truly this was the forbidden obsession, but I couldn't stop. As I continued putting that particular message together, it was as if the Lord said to me, "There is an answer for you here. What did I tell Joshua to do?" "Go round and round Jericho," I answered. "I didn't tell him to go round and round all day," he replied. "I told him to go round *once* a day and then return to camp and get on with life!"

If I hadn't had to face and overcome a Jericho,
others would still be going round and round their
own Jericho today!

There it was! A practical application that hit me like a ton of bricks. God gave me permission—no, rather orders—to go round my particular Jericho *once a day*. Once a day I was to wait on the Lord and pray about my Jericho—this impossible thing in the path of my life! Then I was to leave it to him and return to camp. Others needed me. My family, though understanding and patient, looked to me for help they weren't getting because, although I was with them in body, I was absent in mind!

I began being obedient—going round Jericho once a day and then for the next twenty-four hours refusing to go round and round my problem again. The gloom lifted. Oh, the concern remained—Jericho still stood overshadowing my days. It was still there, dark and forbidding at the edge of the camp, but I was different. And my camp was different because I was.

As I began to teach that particular lesson from the life of Joshua all over the world, other worriers were helped with the lessons I had learned. And you know, little by little I began to be really happy about that. Why, if I hadn't had to face and overcome a Jericho, others would still be going round and round their own Jericho today!

How to Sing under the Gloom Tree

At the back of my Bible I have a little formula to stop me from hanging up my harp on the gloom tree. It's quite simple in principle but very hard to practice. It says:

Here is a problem. I need to pray:

(a) "Give me your mind on this matter,

(b) direct me in prayer to this end,

(c) meet me in Scripture and help me apply it,

(d) forbid me to worry. Amen."

Seek God's mind on the matter.

Now we must believe he is active in the situation despite all evidence to the contrary, and we must mind our own business and stop wanting to govern his universe, of which we are such an infinitesimal part!

We need to set our compasses in his direction. As soon as trouble hits and worry leaps up to respond, we must ask him, "What is your mind on this matter, Lord?" We need to say, "Give me your thoughts, and help me respond in a way that pleases you. Tell me only what you know I need to understand, and let me be content with that."

I have found it helpful to ask a mature Christian friend to give me input when things seem foggy, and a Christian bookstore is a great place to visit, too. There are books on every subject by competent authors, and God may affirm your direction as you read one of them.

Mix your reading with prayer.

As I meet him in prayer, he will direct me as to the very prayers he wants me to pray. On my face, on my knees—in my waiting room—I must expect a personal encounter with my God to this end. As I learn to hurl my anxieties on him in prayer, I will see my soul strangely lightened. Unless we can pray to release our worries rather than simply replay them, we will not have an open and receptive mind to hear the voice of God. I have found it helpful to use a worship tape to prepare my prayer time. Meditation on a verse is good preparation as well. We rush into the presence of God sometimes, gobble on about our Jericho, and then go on our way again without ever giving God a chance to speak to us. That's a bit like paying a visit to the doctor, spending all the time telling him your symptoms, then leaving! A time of stillness and quietness before coming to the Scripture can be great preparation.

Look for specific ways to apply Scripture.

I have a little black notebook, and when a problem arises, I write a "headline" about it. Then, as I am in the Scripture daily, I keep an eye out for anything that relates to that particular need. When I come upon a verse of Scripture that applies, I write it down in that little black book. When we were busy with youth evangelism in England (before we immigrated to the States), some of the young people we got to know asked us to visit their friends and tell them about the Lord. The problem was that their friends were in the pubs and strip joints! I began to worry about people seeing me going into these places. What would they think about me? They might not understand what our motivation was.

I put the question down in my little black book: "Should I go with the kids this weekend?" That week I kept my question in the back of my mind as I had my time with God. Daily, it seemed, I read relevant Scriptures, principles, or commands that directly related. For example, one day I was reading in the book of Philippians. I read how Jesus made a great journey from heaven to hell. A great journey of grace for me so I could go to heaven. He "made himself of no reputation," I read. Well now that was to the point! I applied it to my question. If Jesus made himself of no reputation for me in order that I could have my sins forgiven and go to heaven, then surely I could make myself of no reputation and go into those places to tell them about it. If he made a great journey of grace for me, I could make a little journey in grace and go for him.

Other pieces of Scripture confirmed that thought. One day I read the story of Jesus telling some Pharisees who were raising questions about the company he kept, "I didn't come to save the righteous but sinners!" Then on the Friday before the Saturday we were to go with the kids, I read, "Go into all the world and preach the gospel to every creature." That did it! I had no doubts which part of my world was my responsibility. And so we went and began ten years of evangelism that reaped a great harvest of young people for the kingdom of God.

> *We will find ourselves believing he is active on our behalf, despite perhaps all evidence to the contrary.*

As we go out into our world to face our Jerichos, we will find ourselves believing he is active on our behalf, despite perhaps all evidence to the contrary. Then there will be peace. In the end it is the knowledge that worry is sin that will help me most of all. "Whatever is not of faith is sin," the Bible tells me. A big part of worry is emotion, and I can't do too much about telling my emotions what to do; but worry is also sin, and I know what to do about that. I need to repent. I must stop sinning. Jesus died and rose again in order that we won't need to sin anymore, and that means Jesus died and rose again so we don't need to worry anymore! Oh, joy! Now we can recognize the sin of worry for what it is—a lack of trust in an utterly trustworthy God! As I take no thought for tomorrow, I will discover tomorrow taking thought for the things of itself (Matt. 6:34).

The Message renders this verse: "Give your entire attention to what God is doing right now, and don't get worked up about what may or may not happen tomorrow. God will help you deal with whatever hard things come up when the time comes." I have come to accept the fact that what God is doing right now in most of our lives is allowing enough worries to come our way to worry us into his arms, to grow us up and teach us trust, and to give us songs of faith and joy to sing along in the pathway and the darkest tunnels of all!

> *Trust Him when thy wants are many;*
> *Trust Him when thy friends are few;*
> *And the time of swift temptation*
> *Is the time to trust Him, too.*
>
> *Trust Him when thy soul is burden'd*
> *With the sense of all its sin;*
> *He will speak the word of pardon,*
> *He will make thee clean within.*
>
> *Trust Him for the grace sufficient,*
> *Ever equal to thy need;*
> *Trust Him always for the answer,*
> *When in His dear name you plead.*
>
> *Trust Him for the grace to conquer;*
> *He is able to subdue;*
> *Trust Him for the power for service;*
> *Trust Him for the blessing, too.*
>
> *Trust Him when dark doubts assail thee,*
> *Trust Him when thy strength is small,*
> *Trust Him when to simply trust Him*
> *Seems the hardest thing of all.*
>
> *Trust Him; He is ever faithful;*
> *Trust Him; for His will is best;*

Trust Him; for the heart of Jesus
Is the only place of rest.

Trust Him, then, through cloud or sunshine,
All thy cares upon Him cast;
Till the storm of life is over,
And the trusting days are past.
—The Keswick Hymnbook (p. 102)

LEARNING TO SING AGAIN

SPENDING TIME TOGETHER
For couples, families, Bible study groups, Sunday school classes, or for family devotions

1. Read Philippians 4:6-7. Find a warning, command, and promise in these verses.

2. Look up the following verses of Scripture, and make a list of the particular worries they talk about.

- Luke 12:11-12
- Luke 12:25
- 1 Corinthians 7:32
- Psalm 39:6
- Luke 10:40
- Luke 12:29

3. Discuss any practical way you have helped yourself not to worry.

4. Which part of the chapter helped you and why?

5. Pray together using Philippians 4:6-7.

SPENDING TIME ALONE

Think of a problem you have. Then find a quiet place, and work through the following formula:

1. Specify the problem to the Lord.

2. Ask him to give you his thoughts on the matter.

3. Invite the Holy Spirit to create the right prayers to pray. Pray them.

4. Open your Bible to a psalm. Read until you find a relevant principle, promise, command, or warning.

5. Thank him for the direction he has given you.

6. Leave the thing with him. *Don't* take it out the door of your prayer time with you.

7. Practice trust. Decide to believe that he is and that he will be active in this situation despite all evidence to the contrary.

8. Sing a song! (You will probably need to be alone to do this!)

9. Share the benefits of this time with

- an "Israelite"—another believer

- a "Babylonian"—someone who doesn't know Christ

10. Now it's time to choose another problem to practice on!

CHAPTER EIGHT

THE "GIRL" TREE

Free yourself from the chains on your neck,
O captive Daughter of Zion.
Isaiah 52:2

The Lord has made proclamation to the ends of the earth:
"Say to the Daughter of Zion, 'See, your Savior comes!'"
Isaiah 62:11

For many of the women who found themselves sitting by the river Chebar during the captivity, the possibility of joy was a pipe dream. To begin with, the Babylonians had a pretty low view of their own women, let alone women slaves from other cultures. To quote Gilbert and Sullivan: "A woman's lot was 'not a happy one—happy one!'"

A woman's identity crisis began way back in the Garden of Eden. It was Eve who began to wonder who she was and why she was who she was. Egged on by the serpent, she decided to use her privileged freedom of choice to write a personal declaration of independence. Then she persuaded Adam, her counterpart, to do the same. At this point her relationships spun out of control, and she experienced first shame and then blame. Sin always leads to hiding, and the Lord God, walking alone in the cool of the evening the day the human race began to die, asked, "Where are you?" He might also have asked, "Who are you?" for he knew that Eve's identity crisis had begun. Eve must have shivered behind her tree—even though the evening would have been warm—for she realized the eyes of a holy and righteous God had seen it all. She was soon to find out what God thought about her, what Adam thought about her, and what she thought about herself.

It was Eve who began to wonder who she was and why she was who she was.

"What have you done?" God wanted to know—not that he was ignorant—he was just inviting confession and repentance in order to forgive, restore, and remake Eve's broken image.

"The snake made me do it," Eve offered defensively. We've heard that one before, haven't we? Adam, not to be outdone in the blame game, chipped in with "The woman thou gavest me made me do it." (We've heard that one, too.)

"You both did it—and now it's done!" replied the Lord God. What was done could not be undone, but God would find a way to "cover" their transgressions. Surely just as he made animal skins to cover a new shame that they felt was now connected to their sexuality, God would provide a way of forgiveness—a garment of salvation that would cover and atone for their willful disobedience and the disastrous results of the Fall.

The Fall's Consequences to Women

From that time to this, the daughters of Eve have been hanging up their harps on the "woman" tree. No joy to belong to our sex, they say. As a result of the Fall, headship turned into subjugation, and many, many women down the ages have felt enslaved by the role imposed on them by a male-dominated society and, in large measure, the church. Listen to the sentiments of Tertullian, an early church father writing on the spirit of Eve:

You are the devil's gateway. You are the unsealer of the [forbidden] tree. You are the first deserter of the divine law. You are she who persuaded him whom the devil was not valiant enough to attack. You destroyed so easily God's image man. On account of your desert (i.e., punishment) that is death, even the Son of God had to die.

That doesn't make Eve's daughters feel very good about themselves, does it?

But what of today? If you belong to the female part of the human race in this latter part of the twentieth century, what do you think about your gender? Is there joy in it or sorrow? Jonathan Cape said, "There is no subject more charged with passion than the relation between the sexes. In one way or another it lies behind most of the poetry and most of the crime, most of the sublimity and most of the cruelty, most of the ecstasy and most of the boredom in all of our lives." So how do men see women, and women see men? What do women think of themselves today? Most important, what does Jesus think about women, for therein lies joy for the daughters of Eve!

Jesus and Women

Women were the first to be present at Jesus' birth, the last present at Jesus' crucifixion, and the first to be given the incredible privilege of sharing the great and good news of the Resurrection. Throughout his life Jesus treated women with great respect and dignity, addressing one lady who came for help as a "daughter of Abraham." This was quite revolutionary for the culture of the day. "Sons" of Abraham there may well be, but "daughters" of Abraham? Whoever had conceived of such a thing!?

In a day and time when the Orthodox Jew would include in his morning prayers, "I thank thee God, I am not a slave, I am not a Gentile, I am not a woman," Jesus made firm friends and followers of slaves, Gentiles, and women! In Christ, a slave could become the Lord's freedman. In a day when slaves, children, and women often shared the same treatment, a Gentile woman could seek help and healing from Christ for her stricken child. Women from all levels of society were involved in Christ's life and ministry. They ranked among the Lord's closest earthly friends (Mary and Martha) and assisted and traveled with him on his tours of ministry, helping to support him out of their own means (Luke 8:1-3).

> *As a result of the Fall, headship turned into subjugation, and many, many women down the ages have felt enslaved by the role imposed on them by a male-dominated society and, in large measure, the church.*

Women who were sinners found forgiveness, women who were sick found health, and women who were dead found life! Jesus afforded women the highest honor when he allowed—rather called—Mary and Martha to sit at his feet and learn, an unthinkable invitation to most who watched, including the male disciples. The rabbinical comment on such radical departure of the normal treatment of the fairer sex was "Better to give the Torah to a dog, than to a woman!" And here was the Lord Jesus, the Rabbi—the Teacher—rebuking Martha for being distracted from learning of him by her expected serving role and womanly duties in the kitchen! Jesus was indeed a revolutionary! When you read the Gospels, you cannot but be amazed at Christ's attitude and treatment of women in an age when females were regarded as the "darker sex"—a woman being treated not as the deceived but as the deceiver! There is every reason in the world to hang up your harp on the girl tree if your experience and treatment as a woman has fallen victim of any of these negative attitudes.

A lot of this depends on whether you view Genesis 3:16 as a prescriptive statement or a descriptive one. It reads: "Then he said to the woman, 'You will bear children with intense pain and suffering. And though your desire will be for your husband, he will be your master.'" If you look at that little phrase "he will be your master" as a prescription God wrote for men in order to keep women in their place and prevent them from deceiving and causing men to sin, then you will, in all probability, take a hierarchical stance when it comes to the relationship of men and women. If you take that little phrase as descriptive, then you will take the viewpoint that God, knowing all things in advance, was describing a dark future for women down through the ages who he knew would suffer subjugation as a result of the Fall. If you take this point of view, you will lean toward a more egalitarian (not the same as liberationist) stance. You will probably believe the man's headship is to be exercised in order to make sure the woman is equal!

It makes me feel very tenuous about my gender to know some men look upon my sex as the deceivers and the ones through whom sin entered and poisoned the race.

It makes me feel very tenuous about my gender to know some men look upon my sex as the deceivers and the ones through whom sin entered and poisoned the race. Doesn't it say as in "Adam" all die—and not as in "Eve" (1 Cor. 15:22)? Male and female were equally responsible, and man—male and female—can be equally repentant and redeemed. In *Split Image,* Ann Atkins points out that men and women were created equally good after God's likeness and were "equally culpable" when they were equally bad. "It is wrong," she says, "to suggest the woman was more sinful than the man!" Romans 6:23 tells us we are both—male and female—equally responsible and equally answerable for our self-willed rebellion against God. But—oh, joy—we can all be equally saved! And what a salvation is ours! In Christ, all barriers and battles are dealt with, for in him "there is neither Jew nor Greek, slave nor free, male nor female, for you are all one in Christ Jesus" (Gal. 3:28).

God can mend my broken image—my mirror image of God's likeness written in my character and on my soul. When I recognize the Eve in me and ask Christ to forgive me and enter my life by his Spirit, my femininity will begin to reflect his likeness, and other people will see him!

> *Mirror image spoiled by sin,*
> *Mourn I what you might have been.*
> *Sin caused me to hide in shame,*
> *To put on others my own blame.*
> *Oh, make my broken image new,*
> *And tell me what I need to do.*
>
> *When the risen Christ is come*
> *To my heart to make it home,*
> *He in me will change my life,*
> *And whether single, or a wife,*
> *Will help my soul thy likeness bear*
> *So my lost world may see you there!*
> —J.B.

When a woman finds her joy in the Lord and doesn't search for that joy in a man, woman, or child, she will find her heartstrings dancing whatever her earthly relationships are like. Her joy will be in the fact she reflects the mirror image of the one she loves supremely.

A Shared Song: Hannah and Mary

Think of Hannah. She had a godly husband, Elkanah, who favored her over his second wife, Peninnah. Despite the fact Hannah was childless, she had a husband, a good man who loved her. He would ask her, "Don't I mean more to you than ten sons?" (1 Sam. 1:8). At this point of her story Hannah was finding no joy in her difficult marriage and was looking for joy in motherhood—a motherhood that lay tantalizingly out of her reach.

It was not until Hannah left her longings at God's throne that her soul began to tap-dance! The Scripture says, "Her face was no longer downcast" (1 Sam. 1:18). After committing the whole matter to God, Hannah was granted her heart's wish, and little Samuel was born. Then Hannah composed music indeed! We have a record of the song she sang the day she took that treasured child to the temple, keeping her vow to God and Eli that he should be brought up there under the priest's training! "My heart rejoices in the Lord," she sang (1 Sam. 2:1)—and she could well have added, "And not in my circumstances!" A woman's joy lies first and foremost in the Lord and her relationship with him.

It's no surprise at all to me to find Mary borrowing Hannah's hymn when she visited Elizabeth hundreds of years later. Mary's joy was not dependent on her relationship with Joseph—or her harp would have remained hanging in the tree by her turbulent river of Babylon! Her relationship with Joseph was at that moment in shreds. Her joy, like Hannah's, had its source in the God she loved above all else and the one birthed by the Holy Spirit within her: God in embryo—a baby boy in the making (Luke 1:47-55).

Mary's sense of worth as a woman had been affirmed by one of God's mightiest angels when one glorious morning he visited her and said, "Greetings, you who are highly favored!" or "Good morning! You're beautiful with God's beauty. Beautiful inside and out! God be with you" (Luke 1:28, *The Message*). Oh, Lord, what a morning that must have been! It was the dawn of a new day for women everywhere who had been treated with ignominy. Mary found her deepest joy and sang her sweetest song that day. She found her delight in being a "heartmaid" and a handmaid of the Lord! (v. 38, KJV). Any woman willing to live a "may it be to me" life, as Mary was willing to do, will fill her soul with notes of the deepest fulfillment. When a handmaid of the Lord begins a joyful pilgrimage along the road to heaven, the obedience it requires will not be found onerous.

So finding joy means first of all finding Jesus—or rather allowing Jesus to find us! We must stop hiding and playing the blame game. When we stop hiding, we'll stop hurting. When we listen to God's words to us, women that we are, and like Mary say, "May it be to me as you have said," the symphony will begin.

Mary, the handmaid of the Lord, was also a heartmaid of the Lord. "She treasured up all these things [things concerning Jesus] and pondered them in her heart" (Luke 2:19). She "kept all these things," the King James Version tells us. That's something women are very good at doing: keeping things. We treasure and hoard things that are precious to us. We women are collectors—just come and peek into our attics! What we collect, of course, tells you something about who we are!

Mary, a handmaid and a heartmaid of the Lord, collected words others spoke about Jesus and held these things dearly and deeply within herself. No wonder we find her singing a song to Elizabeth! What does God think about women who are like Mary? He thinks they are really worth something! Not only does he think they were worth creating, he thinks they are worth saving, teaching, training, discipling, commissioning, and sending.

When Jesus was saying his earthly good-byes, he told the twelve disciples to "go into all the world and preach the good news to all creation" (Mark 16:15). Nobody believes he meant that only those twelve men were to do this. There were 120 men and women in the upper room at Pentecost. They were men and women waiting together to be empowered and equipped to see visions, dream dreams, and preach the gospel to every nation beginning at Jerusalem. The fire fell on men and women alike. The flames did not skip over female heads and alight on male heads only! All spoke in tongues—enabling everyone in Jerusalem to hear and understand the gospel and take it home with them all over the known world. That commissioning continues to this present day.

When I think of the wonder of women discovering their spiritual birthright, I think of the story of Elizabeth Mittelstaedt, whose impact on her world of women is recounted in the last chapter of this book. Her birth—a miracle in itself—and her family's difficult circumstances led her to think little of herself and of her womanhood.

Elizabeth was nearly aborted because her mother, who was very ill and living under communist rule where medicines were hard to come by, was encouraged by her doctor to abort the child rather than have it born infected. Yet, a strange sense of foreboding gripped her heart, and she seemed to hear a voice say, "Don't kill this baby!" She did not know the God who spoke to her, yet she heeded his silent voice. A few months later she delivered a sickly little girl and named her Elizabeth.

When Elizabeth was nine years old, Maria and her family heard the gospel, and they all accepted Christ. In her teens, after hearing a woman missionary speak, Elizabeth promised God that if he ever needed another woman to serve him, she would be that woman. Miraculously, God opened doors for her to attend Bible college, where she prepared for ministry and met the man she would marry.

Several years later a flawed dental procedure left Elizabeth in constant, excruciating pain. One day as she was walking across a bridge over a small river in her town, she looked down into the water, and a voice seemed to say, "Jump!"

Startled, she looked up and across the bridge to the pretty little German village beyond with its geranium flower boxes and white picket fences. "Behind those nice homes there is a lot of pain and brokenness for women," she heard God say to her.

"I could feel how God loves the women," Elizabeth recalls. "In that moment my heart was broken about what broke his heart. So I said, 'God, I would love to help, but what can I do?'"

That was the day God gave her the idea of a magazine for women. A truly preposterous idea! Publishers were sure that German women wouldn't read it and no one would finance it. But her husband encouraged her. And when she cried out to God, "You see, God, nobody wants this magazine," she heard him saying, "But I want it!"

Shortly thereafter, the frail little child who had been rescued from the abortionist's knife by the voice of the God her mother did not yet know, became the editor of *Lydia* magazine. Contrary to all the warnings publishers had given her, the magazine had a circulation of ten thousand by the third issue. Today it is published in German, Romanian, and Hungarian and read by an estimated one million readers.

Elizabeth is a handmaid of the Lord. She celebrates her womanhood. Being a handmaid and a heartmaid, however, doesn't mean you won't be a hurt maid! Mary experienced a sword piercing her own heart as she watched Jesus crucified. But that hurt was transformed on the other side of the Cross. Serving Jesus is worthwhile, and joy truly comes in the morning. Mary, Jesus' beloved mother, was in the upper room at Pentecost when the Holy Spirit came in power, and for the second time she was overshadowed and indwelt by him.

A Song of Singleness

Some of you single women may say, "But Mary and Joseph did manage to get things sorted out and had a pretty good relationship after the dust settled. I'm single—and you can't tell me the joy of the Lord makes up for that! I don't believe I can be a single woman and be happy."

There were many single women in the early church. In the New Testament culture a father had the right to give or withhold his daughters in marriage. Many gave their girls, but many didn't.

Paul addresses this in his letter to the church in Corinth. Remember, at the end of the first century, marriage customs were so different from ours that it's hard to draw parallels and applications to our life now—but some principles still pertain.

In 1 Corinthians 7 Paul calls both men and women,
married or single, to single-mindedness.

Paul was living in difficult and dangerous days. It was life-threatening to be a Christian man or woman! Persecution had broken out, and Paul himself was to lose his life during the reign of the notorious emperor Nero. Because the days were so dangerous, Paul advised Christian fathers to think twice before arranging marriages for their daughters. It would be quite possible that wives or children would be tortured, thrown to the lions, or tarred and set alight as human torches for one of Nero's dinner parties in order to force Christian husbands or fathers to recant. Paul wanted to spare people this agony.

But he also spoke positively of the state of singleness for the woman who, for whatever reason, was not given in marriage. In so doing, he gave us a portrait of a woman who could find joy in her celibacy.

Such an idea is almost unheard of in some Christian circles today. Singleness is thought of as a cross to bear, not a state to celebrate. Again, a woman's identity needs to be found in all its fullness in her relationship to God, not in any earthly relationship. In 1 Corinthians 7 Paul calls both men and women, married or single, to single-mindedness. He believed the urgency of the days in which they were living demanded that "those who have wives should live as if they had none" (v. 29). He wasn't for a moment suggesting that husbands neglect or abandon their responsibilities to their wives but rather that their focus and priorities be ordered with the present crisis and the imminent return of the Lord in mind (vv. 20, 29). If this was the case, then, how much more is it today, "for the coming of the Lord is nearer now than when we first believed" (Rom. 13:11, TLB). The apostle urged both men and women to make the most of the moment—to optimize their opportunities apart or together for kingdom thinking, planning, working, and serving to get the job done.

With this in mind he speaks to the women whose choices were being made for them. He says some radical things. He says that singleness is good (1 Cor. 7:7-8). Singleness is a gift. How can singleness be a gift? you ask. Because your singleness opens up the opportunity to "attend upon the Lord without distraction" (KJV) so that "you may live in a right way in undivided devotion to the Lord" (v. 35)—something a married woman finds more difficult.

There is no question that there are distractions attached to the marriage relationship. Paul says a married woman's time and energy are taken up figuring out how she can please her husband, with little free time left over to figure out how to please the Lord (vv. 32-34)!

Paul says that the single woman is "happier if she stays as she is" (v. 40). Paul, who appears to be single, says that he had learned the secret of being content in any situation (Phil. 4:12)—even, I presume, in the state of singleness! Apparently we can learn how to be single, and as we do so, we will learn how to be content. Singleness can even be a privilege and not, as many look upon it, a punishment. In other words, God can help us be glad in the single state instead of getting in a state about our singleness.

So many women have lost their joy right here at the single tree. They spend their days composing internal and eternal dirges about it. They mourn their losses continually. One girl said to me, "I feel as though I am going through the grief process—denial, bargaining, anger, guilt, and trying to push through to acceptance." I asked her about that, and we talked through her grieving experience.

"I'm through the denial stage," she said. "I used to go around putting the best face on my singleness, saying, 'I love being single.' I declared publicly I was willing to be single, but privately—if I was honest—I was planning to be double! That's denial," she added emphatically. "I wasn't willing to tell myself the truth!

"The next stage," she continued, "was bargaining."

"I've heard lots of women do that," I said. "They start off saying, 'Who'll I have,' then move to 'Who'll have me—and end up saying, 'Please Lord, send somebody quick!' I've heard women (and I did it myself once) start bargaining with the Lord: 'I'll do anything—even offer for missions, if you'll give me a partner, Lord!'"

My companion laughed. "I've done that—and I've also been through the anger stage."

"The 'It's not fair, Lord,' bit?" I inquired.

"Right—the bittersweet pain when friend after friend gets engaged, and I find myself a bridesmaid one more time!" she said ruefully.

"What about the guilt stage?"

"The 'Is it my fault? I wonder what's wrong with me' part? I'm just about done with the 'I must be weird' or even 'They must be weird not to want me.' Actually," she continued, "I'm through to acceptance—though only just. I'm working on thinking of singleness as an opportunity to get to know God better than I ever could if I was married with a horde of 'little distractions' around my feet." She stopped, then smiled a beautiful smile. "I know in my head Jesus is all I need—and I guess I can't really experience the good of it all until deep in my heart, Jesus is all I've got!"

Discovering the joy of being the Lord's heartmaid deals with the issue of feeling like a half-maid because you're not married! God can create such a sense of completion in your life when you accept whatever state you find yourself in at this very moment. It's then that you become free to discover solo gifts with which to bless the Babylonians and Israelites.

Have you lost your joy at the girl tree? There are single songs that the Holy Spirit can teach you to play upon your heartstrings if you'll dare to ask him to.

Esther's Song

In the Old Testament we can read the story of Esther. Her history had been one of sorrow and loss. Caught up in the captivity, she found herself chosen to compete in a beauty queen contest. She had no choice at all in the matter. After all, she was a foreign slave—and she was a woman! Suddenly, her entire future was determined, and her own dreams of marriage and family were undoubtedly dashed. What thoughts went through her mind when she was chosen to be queen of Persia? Even as royalty, Esther would be forced to play out a role she'd had no role in creating.

Esther—whose name means "star"—could have hung up her joy early on when she was orphaned and taken prisoner, but she didn't. She sang a song of purity, piety, and poise that made her captors gasp. It was her sweet song of Zion spirituality. Although her masters understood it only dimly, her song won her the queen's crown—a doubtful privilege, but one Esther set about using to God's advantage. Esther persevered. She refused to be or do anything less than her best for the God she served.

After Esther was made queen, the Jews fell victim to a plot conceived by a Jew hater named Haman. He intended to destroy them. Esther was reminded by her godly uncle Mordecai, who had raised her, that God had surely brought her to the throne "for such a time as this." Esther came to the crossroads of her faith. She, too, was a Jew—though the king and his cronies didn't know that. She had a choice to declare it and risk death herself or stay silent and perhaps save her own life. Would she allow the Lord to play the heartstrings of her life and let the whole world know whose she was and whom she served? Or would her harp remain silent and still?

With trembling heart but willing will, Esther chose obedience.

She and her maidservants waited on the Lord, and the whole of the Jewish nation, alerted to the deadly crisis, fasted, prayed, and waited with her. Then, taking her life in her hands—or more accurately, placing it in God's hands—she went to plead with the king for her people. You can read the words of her song in the record. It was a strong song. It was a sweet and brave song. It was also a battle song. It was a song sung as only a daughter of Zion—a daughter of *the* King—could sing it! And it won the day! It was a saving song sung by a woman, and it saved the entire Jewish population in that place.

She sang a song of purity, piety, and poise that made her captors gasp.

If you are a woman, you can be glad you are a woman! There are so many reasons to rejoice about it. More reasons for joy than sorrow, more reasons for praise than pain! A woman's identity revealed in creation, obscured in the Fall, and renewed in redemption means Holy Spirit privilege and responsibilities for each of us "daughters of Eve." To be a daughter of Eve saved by God's grace, a daughter of Zion gifted to witness, and a daughter of the King is privilege enough to sing a song of glory—all day long—and all the way home!

Learning New Songs

When I came to America, I wasn't really sure I wanted to sing a song about my womanhood. However, being a brand-new pastor's wife threw me into the struggle of realizing my femininity was a God-given gift for ministry to women. I was in my midforties, and having left a vibrant and satisfying youth ministry, I wrestled with a new focus. God used other women in my life to teach me a new song—a song of celebration I never dreamed I would still be singing decades later.

I began to believe I should have stuck with ministering to teenagers, where my gifts had been tried and trained. How had I gotten into this situation in the first place? It wasn't hard to find the answer. If your husband is a speaker, I discovered, the public expects you to be able to follow suit. All sorts of doors of opportunity had opened up to me as soon as I had arrived in the States, simply because of Stuart's already well-established ministry.

"But I don't want to speak to women," I complained to the Eternal One. He knew I never had liked it when lots of women were compressed together in a confined space. What a row they made, for starters! But, having learned not to be a Jonah and run away from my responsibility to speak to people I didn't particularly like, I had answered the invitation and gone anyway. *It really doesn't matter that I don't like them very much,* I thought. After all, they needn't know. Just like Jonah, I marched into Nineveh (the situation I would like to have marched away from) and preached my heart out, retiring like that same angry prophet to my hill of disdain once the engagement was over. But God apparently used the message, and I received requests to return.

Then one day I went to Memphis, Tennessee. Verla met me at the airport. She was a speaker and teacher, ran a rescue mission, talked to up-and-outers and down-and-outers, and was totally relaxed with both. She gave me an uncomfortable feeling in the pit of my conscience the moment I saw her warm touch with the women. We completed our meetings, and she was very appreciative of my part, but everything she felt about me came right through her transparent personality. Or maybe she didn't feel like that at all, and it was just that her whole approach and ministry served to rebuke me outright, saying louder than any verbal complaint, "Jill, you are technically a good speaker—*but* you do not love these women!"

Seeing the love of God in action in Verla's life made me want it for myself. It seemed such a very simple thing to do to love the women like she did. I told God about my intentions to try and emulate Verla's example. He was very glad to hear the news as he had—unknown to me—thousands more women for me to meet. From that moment on, the Holy Spirit set about shedding abroad his love for them in my heart.

But did this mean I was to love *all* women or just some? I knew I would have no problem at all feeling very much at home at the rescue mission, but what about the "Ultrasuede" women? God could help me to love even them, I decided. But that wasn't the issue; the problem was, would they love me and, most important of all, listen to what I had to tell them? Once I was on my feet with my Bible open and a message prepared, I felt fine. It was the before-and-after bit that got to me—the socializing and the small talk—the winning-of-the-women-to-myself-that-I-might-win-them-to-him part. Just as I knew the teens had needed to like me first in order to listen to what I had to say, I knew the ground had to be cleared with these sophisticated, clever American women before I ever got up behind my security blanket of a pulpit. What I was like off the platform was a question those girls had every right to ask. If they knew my insecurities, if they heard my foolish attempts at making classy conversation, I knew they would dislike me. I groaned aloud, thinking of the disappointment the women were in for as they found out there was nothing to me after all.

Freed from Competition

And then one day the Eternal One decided it was time to set me free. I was in Coral Gables, Florida, among some of the nouveau riche young women who populated that classy area of Miami. Observing them as they entered the club restaurant where we were dining, I noticed that each one seemed a beauty in her own lovely right. Sitting at a table with three of the most elegant females, I felt fat, forty, and somewhat futile. Why, oh why, had I come? As my companions ate minute portions of diet dessert and I nervously attacked my pecan pie, I remembered Erma Bombeck saying, "When your dog gives you strange looks when you get out of the shower, it's time to do something about your weight." It wasn't the dog giving me the strange looks this time, I thought grimly.

I looked around at the beautiful exclusive-like creature who had just made her entrance—from an exclusive car—into that exclusive place and was about to order some of their exclusive food at a definitely exclusive price. Suddenly and unexpectedly the Eternal One inquired of me, "Why do you think everyone is so tense?"

I discovered myself in a still point. "Competition," I replied with sudden comprehension. "That's right," he answered. It was very, very still in my heart, and so I very distantly heard the Eternal One's next words: "Jill, you'll *never* be competition."

That was it—I was free. Oh, the joy of it! It was true. I could be a big sister to them, a friendly mother to them, an ugly aunt to them. But I could relax now, knowing I would never threaten one of them. They were bound to listen to me for the very reason I had believed them bound not to. What an incredible release!

God had made me just right for my vocation, and that was all that mattered. He had gifted me with ordinary and acceptable good looks. Everywhere I went someone would always come up to me and tell me I was like their daughter, cousin, or Great-Aunt Susan. Now I could see how comfortable that made everybody feel. Why, I was as familiar as family, and instead of being offended by these remarks, conjuring up freaky pictures of Great-Aunt Frankenstein Susan, I was able to giggle and be content! I thanked God for dressing me well enough to hold my own, but not too well to distract or cause envy, freeing me up in that moment of time to wear an outfit twice in a row if I wanted to and not be trapped in an expensive game of "beat the fashion." For the first time I was able to be glad for my fine hair, realizing that because it curled so easily, I could always bully it into shape, and instead of majoring on my minors, I began to make a mental list of my best qualities.

I did have a sort of pleasant voice (that made a long talk partway enjoyable), an expressive face (useful for dramatic emphasis), and a metabolism that could be mastered by diet and discipline. To discover you are "just right" in his eyes is enough. He is the lover of our soul, and to despise the way he has assembled our body, dressed our head with foliage, or arranged our features is to miss the point. To be able to say, "I am free not to be the 'me' that 'I' would choose to be, but the me 'he' has already chosen me to be," is freedom indeed.

I took time out to meet with and listen to God in that particular waiting room, and with the memory of Coral Gables fresh in my mind, the Eternal One again applied his Word to my heart. He reminded me of some of the deliverances he had already given me: the way he had overcome my fear of losing friends, of sharing my faith, of being attacked on the back streets of Liverpool. The fear of something happening to the children or to Stuart and the horror of rejection and death. He had dealt with the apprehension of adjusting to our new environment and the awful fear of flying. He had visited me with the written living Word, and it had proved to be sweeter than honey, finer than gold, more precious than rubies. Even my fearful obediences had brought me great reward. They had led to marvelous adventures that I wouldn't have missed for anything.

As I knelt, the Father dressed my spirit with an incredibly tender anticipation of heavenly delight, and I told the Lord Jesus how much I loved him for it all.

Shuffling through my invitations in the weeks that followed and with a quickening excitement, I chose three of the most challenging I had ever been given and wrote an eager acceptance. Surprised by peace and with an incredible new hope, I breathed—West Point, Princeton, Washington . . . ultra, Ultrasuede women—here we come. And as I went it was with the prayer of Psalm 19:14 uppermost in my thinking: "May the words of my mouth and the meditation of my heart be pleasing in your sight, O Lord, my Rock and my Redeemer."

As I stood on platforms here and there and felt wooden planks or shiny bricks underneath my feet, I somehow knew I would begin to feel another substance undergirding my obediences—*my Rock.* That new confidence in my Redeemer's promises would begin to work in me a new sense of well-being with myself.

When I got to Washington, I noticed fashions must have changed. I couldn't see any Ultrasuede around. Then I looked a little closer and found it was there all the time. It wasn't even Ultrasuede, but ultra, ultra, ultra. At last I was seeing the people in it, and they, I found, were just like everyone else. As I sought to have words from the Eternal One that were acceptable in his sight, I found they accepted them, too. I could even table-hop around the exclusive restaurants, chat about anything or nothing at the reception, and enjoy it all. What a life!

My ministry took on a new swing—an exuberance, a depth of satisfaction and sureness I'd never known before. Flying outside to catch a plane to the next assignment, I smiled at the jumble of cars and at my frantic hostess, running around like a scalded cat—she couldn't remember where she'd parked. I was reminded of my husband's quip: "Women don't park cars; they abandon them!" The next time some dear little blue-haired ladies in tennis shoes came and whispered in my ear, "We couldn't hear you," and I asked, "Where were you sitting?" and they answered me, "On the back row and we're all deaf, you know," I found a sweet warmth and loving concern instead of the old irritation as I patiently suggested they sit in the front row next time!

It was all different. Women were everywhere. In my head and in my heart, in my plans and in my thinking, in my schedules and spare moments, on the phone and in my car, at the restaurant and at tennis, in my tears and in my laughter. They were part of me, and I was part and parcel of them—and I was glad, glad, glad we were women together!

These last twenty years have only underlined my convictions that my identity revealed in creation, lost in the Fall, but renewed in redemption is in Christ and my relationship with him. My celebration of womanhood has been a place of deep joy and service as a handmaid of the Lord. The songs I have learned have been melodies that I have been privileged beyond measure to teach to other women along the way.

Are You under the Girl Tree?

What a joy to learn to sing a song about your womanhood. What relief and release to realize the advantages. Only a woman gets the chance to bear a child. Oh, the joy when a small eternal person is born into the world and motherhood begins. Only a woman can be a wife. What fulfillment to partner with a man in serving the Lord and bringing up godly children to make a significant difference in their own generation. Only a woman can be a grandmother and have the chance to influence and model all over again—without the work of it all!

It was God's design that produced us—God's incredible, wonderful weaving of the fabric of our womanhood in our mother's womb. We are fearfully and wonderfully made—embroidered in color, charm, and character by the Creator himself, who claims to be delighted with his handiwork!

If we are unfortunate enough to have been treated little better than slaves, the victims of negative messages, or worse because of our womanhood, we need to let God treat us as daughters of the King, lovers of Jesus, and servants of the Most High God.

How to Sing When You're under the Girl Tree

- Make a list of all the things you don't like about being a woman, and search God's Word for answers to everything on your list.

- Read some good evangelical books on what it means to be a Christian woman.

- Brainstorm with God, ideas of how to volunteer for things that need to be done in your neighborhood, school district, inner city, or church that a woman would be more likely than a man to do well; e.g., if you've had breast cancer, start a support group in your home or outside it.

- Study the women of the Bible starting with Eve, and make lists of all the good things you can learn about the advantages of being a woman.

- Read Psalm 139, studying it with Bible reference helps.

- Pray about being a woman, alone in the waiting room, or with a group of women discuss these matters.

- Get on with serving the Lord, forgetting your gender.

- Make up a thank-you prayer or poem about your womanhood, and keep it in your Bible to sing when you're discouraged in this matter.

- Take down that harp from the girl tree and join the female Israelites by the waters of this particular river of Babylon—and sing!

LEARNING TO SING AGAIN

SPENDING TIME TOGETHER

For couples, families, Bible study groups, Sunday school classes, or for family devotions

1. For what reasons do women lose their joy today? List five reasons.

2. Share one reason you are glad you are a woman (if you are!).

3. Read the book of Esther. Divide up the chapters, asking members of the group to read a chapter or two to themselves and afterward recount their chapter to the group in their own words.

4. What did Esther's life say

   • to the Israelites?

   • to the Babylonians?

   • to you?

5. Pray for women you know who have hung up their harp on the girl tree.

6. How can the men in your church affirm women and use them in their fellowship?

SPENDING TIME ALONE

1. Read the Genesis account of the creation of woman in Genesis.

2. What three things make you glad you are a woman?

3. Read the Genesis account of the Fall (Gen. 3). What one thing can you identify with in Eve's dilemma?

4. Read Genesis 3:15. Whom does this speak of? What difference would Jesus make for women through his work of redemption?

5. Read Acts 2:1-19; Galatians 3:28.

- What three advantages did Mary, the mother of Jesus, have because she was a woman?

- What advantages do you have?

6. Pray about the above.

CHAPTER NINE

THE GIFT TREE

*God has given each of us
the ability to do certain things well.*

Romans 12:6, NLT

J esus Christ is living in you, and it's his job to save souls," Janet, the girl who led me to Christ, told me the day I became a Christian. "What does saving souls mean?" I asked her, never having heard the expression before. "It means you explain how you became a Christian and help others to do the same," she said. "Oh, I'm no preacher!" I exclaimed. "I'm not very good with words."

"You mean you don't think you're gifted that way?" Janet asked.

"Right," I agreed quickly. "I admire people who have the gift of gab—but it isn't my gift."

"What *is* your gift, Jill?"

I looked at her and couldn't answer. I only hoped telling other people *wasn't* my gift. "I-I can't," I stammered.

"You haven't even tried yet," Janet replied cheerfully. "Here's the night nurse [I was in the hospital]; tell her what happened to you this morning. Let's find out if you can do it or not."

I gazed at her, struck dumb with fright. "How do you know

you can't if you've never tried?" Janet continued insistently. "Jill, if you found the cure for cancer, you'd tell the world, wouldn't you?"

"Of course," I answered. "That's different."

"Is it?" asked my friend. "Isn't the cure for sin, which is eternal, more important than the cure for cancer, which is only temporary?"

"Jill, if you found the cure for cancer, you'd tell the world, wouldn't you?"

"Well, I suppose—"

"Jill, if you really had discovered the cure for cancer, wouldn't you tell everyone, whether you had the gift of gab or not?"

"I suppose so," I admitted reluctantly.

"Here comes the nurse; just start," Janet said in a no-argument sort of voice.

I started. I stumbled and bumbled, and the nurse looked extremely surprised and took my pulse.

"There, you see," I said to Janet accusingly, "she thought I was nuts—I've probably put her off for good!"

In that I was wrong. The next morning as the nurse was doing her rounds before going off duty, she stopped by my bed and said, "Now what were you trying to tell me last night? And where did you learn about it? It sounds interesting." I looked desperately over at Janet, who lay in the next bed gazing studiously at the ceiling. I knew she was refusing to look at me! This time I did a little better—after all, practice makes perfect! When the nurse had taken her leave, Janet asked me, "Happy?"

"Oh yes!" I replied, fingering my heartstrings and looking at the space above my head in the gift tree, where my harp had hung. "Oh yes!"

Looking for Excuses

As the Babylonians demanded gospel songs of the Israelites, the people of God began to make excuses just as I had! "How can we do that?" they cried. "We can't sing! They killed off our best soloists back home in Jerusalem! Anyway, our temple musicians are here to sing, not us." There are many reasons we don't want to sing a gospel song today. And the matter of giftedness often becomes the number one excuse.

We are all specialists in America. Our expertise becomes extremely trained and trimmed until we dare not venture outside our "box": Doesn't the Scripture teach that each one should use the particular spiritual gift God has given him or her and no other? If we were honest we would add, "And, thank goodness, I can't sing a note!" Many Christians have hung up their harps on the gift tree without realizing there are things that need to be done whether we are gifted or not. It's a matter of duty.

Think about it. Some have the gift of giving—yet all must give. Some have the gift of helps—but all God's people must be helpful. Some have the gift of an evangelist—yet all must be witnesses to him. Jesus didn't say to the disciples, "Would you like to be witnesses?" or "If you find the time and you have the gift of gab, would you be my witnesses?" He said, "You *are* witnesses of these things." He told the twelve disciples to "stay in the city until you have been clothed with power from on high" (Luke 24:48-49). Then he said, "You will be my witnesses in Jerusalem, and in all Judea and Samaria, and to the ends of the earth" (Acts 1:8). Notice he did not say, "Wait in Jerusalem until I gift you with gifts," but rather, "until you have been clothed with power"!

There are some things that must be done whether we are gifted or not, and sharing the gospel—being Christ's witnesses—is one of them. For this the gift of power from on high is ours. But we are hard to convince.

"If only I was a really clever speaker, I wouldn't be so shy about trying to reach out to the Babylonians," we say stubbornly. The Babylonians are a wild bunch, and it seems a silly thing to do to sing them a song of any kind if we're not specially gifted. "Why should we stick our neck out? We might well get our head chopped off. Anyway, if it's not my gift, I might do more harm than good."

Notice he did not say, "Wait in Jerusalem until I gift you with gifts," but rather, "till I gift you with power"!

When my husband and I used to work with youth in Europe, we often found ourselves in wild situations. One day a pastor living in a tough town invited my husband to speak to the youth group. When we arrived at the church hall, there was the wildest music pounding out a welcome. As Stuart opened the door, I stood transfixed at the sight of a packed wooden building with kids in total turmoil, gyrating to the deafening beat of the music. I was rooted to the spot. Stuart looked at my white face and said, "Come on, let's do it, Jill. We've got to tell them the truth."

I love my husband's unashamed total commitment to the fact that Christianity isn't just for Christians but for the whole world! The Bible isn't a Judeo-Christian book; it's a book for everybody. As I stood on the steps, my mind racing and my heart beating furiously, I went over the facts of the gospel of Jesus Christ that we would present that night.

We were going to tell them first and foremost that they were sinners. That's scary to begin with. Sinners don't like to be told they're sinners! I remember my own indignation when Janet first told me. Who did this pious, self-righteous girl think she was, calling me a sinner? I was furious! Then she explained the word to me. It really meant "missing the mark." Well that was easier to acknowledge. I knew I'd missed the mark—the mark being the standard of perfection God required of human beings made in his image. So I knew we needed to tell these wild young Babylonians they couldn't go to heaven unless God forgave them for missing the mark, for being sinners.

Sinners don't like to be told they can't go to heaven either! They feel they have the inalienable right to march into heaven any way or anytime they choose. They scoff at the idea that there's only one way through those golden gates and that is through Christ's death on their behalf. "I didn't ask him to die for me," a young girl piped up when my husband got to this part. "I'll find my own way through the pearly gates when it's time, thank you! What makes you jerks think you've got an edge on the truth?" I watched in awe as Stuart patiently and effectively answered that question and many others that night.

As my husband used his God-given gifts to explain the good news that Jesus was the truth about God—the way to heaven and eternal life itself—I coveted his gift. If only I could speak like that! He spoke their language and put lots of illustrations into his talk. I could never do it, I decided! One of the worst boys in that club came to Christ that night. "You never know who's out there just waiting for someone to tell them the truth," Stuart commented. I thought back to the night nurse. That particular boy is in God's service today, and even though he is not eloquent in speech, he is gifted with the conviction that God endues with power from on high those who preach the Good News and honor his Word.

Searching for Our Gifts

There was a time in my life, long after my conversion, when I still honestly believed I did not possess those speaking gifts. Oh, I knew I was a good teacher, but the eloquent creative gifts appeared to me to belong to others. I borrowed my husband's sermons and began memorizing and using them when I was asked to speak in churches. There was one particular sermon on Lazarus that I really enjoyed. I began using it—a lot! One day my husband came home from a five-month-long ministry tour and set off on a Sunday to preach in Manchester. I was busy with the children and cheerily called good-bye as he went out the door. Then I remembered he was going to a church I had been to a month previously, where I had preached his one and only sermon on Lazarus! I had a miserable day hoping he wouldn't use the same one. As soon as he walked through the door, my worst fears were realized. "Lazarus?" I whispered.

"Lazarus!" he answered briefly but eloquently. "Jill, at the end of *my* sermon on Lazarus, a woman came barreling up to me and said accusingly, 'Oooh, you stole your wife's talk!'" At that point my good husband helped me realize I could find my own material and learn how to be creative! The book of Ecclesiastes has a wonderful passage pertaining to gifts (12:9-14). It tells us that "the Teacher [surely one of the wisest, most creative people in the world, namely, Solomon] searched to find just the right words, and what he wrote was upright and true" (v. 10). Words that were wise had come out of a man who had worshiped. They were "given by one Shepherd" (v. 11). But words of worship were also followed by work! The teacher pondered (that is, worried it out, searched, re-searched) and set in order (catalogued) many proverbs. There's a lot of work to be done to hone our creative bent after we have worshiped. So we not only need to witness, whether we have discovered our speaking gift or not, but we have to work hard at developing our speaking effectiveness if we do find out God has indeed given us such abilities. We may well discover a talent or spiritual gift in the executing of our duty to tell our needy world about the Lord. If we do, we can know that one day at the judgment seat we will be held accountable for how we used that gift (v. 14). And it's been my experience that such gifts are often discovered in the simple "doing" and then need to be developed and polished.

Gifts are discovered as we simply meet needs that are often right under our nose.

Gifts are discovered as we simply meet needs that are often right under our nose. It's a good idea to start with our talents. Most people know what their talents are. Talents are those things we received the best grades for in school. The things we enjoy doing the most. The special interests we just somehow found time to pursue as hobbies or recreation. Yes, we can start with our talents.

Israel knew what talents were all about. When they were building the tabernacle in the wilderness, hundreds of people were involved. There were stone masons and weavers and dyers. Those who worked wonders with wood, brass, and clay. There were goldsmiths and silversmiths, carvers and engineers. There were planners and painters. And when it was finished, organizers and administrators. There were singers and teachers, pastors and priests, leaders and followers. The Bible says these craftsmen were filled with the Holy Spirit just as surely as the priests and prophets and prophetesses were (Exod. 35:31). Their talents were talents and their talents were gifts—not for themselves, but for God and his service. Start with a list of your talents, dedicate them to God, and get going working in your local "tabernacle" wherever you see a gap or hole that's a need.

Perhaps you've been hurt or rejected when you've tried to do this in the past. Did you take down your harp and prepare to play a gift and find that the priests didn't want it? Maybe you are part of a fellowship that seems to have someone lined up to do everything already. There's no place for you or your talents and gifts, it seems.

If that is the case, you may want to volunteer for the "army." Not only did Israel need people to build, care for, and work in the tabernacle, there were foes to fight, battles to win, and much land to be possessed. There's always room in the ranks! There are too many people in the church today clamoring to be generals. You could volunteer to be a humble foot soldier. Get out there and do it, for in the doing you may find that you have a knack for the activity you never dreamed you had.

I have the talent and gift of teaching. Yet the mission we served had no place for women teachers at the time we joined. "There's a lost world out there, Jill," my husband advised. "Go get it. You're needed there." And so I became a foot soldier, starting youth groups and halfway houses for youngsters who would never darken the door of a church. And guess what? I found out I could do it! What's more, others recognized that I could do it, too. I got promoted by those who at first had no place for me but who later affirmed me, and soon I was training foot soldiers at the headquarters as well as leading the troops out to the fray! How did I find out I had the gift of an evangelist? I saw a need and set about trying to meet it. I found out in the trying that I could do it. That meant I was gifted and just hadn't known it. As I exercised the gift I hadn't known I had, others acknowledged I had it and invited me to come up higher, which I was delighted to do.

Once we have found out our gifts, we need to polish them. It's like learning to play piano. We won't get better unless we practice. And it's not enough to spiritualize the subject and say we'll just pray about it.

When our youngest child, Peter, chose to join the school orchestra, he decided he wanted to play the drums. We, however, for obvious reasons, decided on the clarinet. Less than enthusiastically, Peter began his musical career. I could not get him to practice. It was like pulling teeth. Toward the end of the semester, Peter came whistling into the kitchen, carrying his instrument on the way to the school bus. "Pray for me today, Mom," he said cheerfully.

"Sure, Peter—what for?"

"Well, we've got tryouts, and I want first-chair clarinet."

"Peter! I can't pray that for you—you haven't practiced in weeks!"

Looking at me with a grin, he replied, "If I'd practiced, I wouldn't need you to pray!"

This, of course, was a teachable moment, which I proceeded to use to explain that prayer wasn't to be used in that way and also gifts and talents need to be polished and perfected.

The church is full of people like our teenage son, cheerfully carrying their gifts and talents to church having hardly practiced, yet expecting to play first-chair clarinet! It doesn't work that way. Training and practice are musts for the people of God who are busy discovering their gifts.

Gifts Still Require Courage

As Stuart's and my youth ministry continued, I realized that although the kids we worked with were a pretty rough bunch, they weren't nearly as dangerous as others beyond the safe confines of church. Outside church, gift or no gift—courage is required! This was brought home to me even this year as I listened to a young boy tell of his adventures in Holland. A team of young believers, both men and women, were trying to witness in a shopping mall in the heart of a city. There's a price to be paid by such brave kids these days if their peers are to hear the gospel.

The young evangelist and his group of friends had taken their puppets and musical instruments along with them. As they sang their contemporary Christian music and prepared to use their puppets to teach biblical truth, a tough street gang circled them. The gang leader pointed to one of his men, and that man came up to the leader of the Christian group and spat in his face. Then the gang leader pointed to the next henchman and the next. They all followed suit until the young follower of Jesus was sitting there with spittle dripping down his face onto his clothes. His mind flew to Isaiah 50:6-7, where the servant of Jehovah is described: "I offered my back to those who beat me, my cheeks to those who pulled out my beard; I did not hide my face from mocking and spitting. Because the Sovereign Lord helps me, I will not be disgraced. Therefore have I set my face like flint, and I know I will not be put to shame." As this young man thought of Jesus—the promised servant about to accomplish our redemption, with spittle pouring down his face as had been prophesied—a great shout of privilege and joy burst out of him. "It's OK," he said to his tormentors. "They did this to my Lord Jesus, you know—so why shouldn't you do it to me?" The gang leader stared at the young man, who calmly began to sing his gospel songs. The bully whirled around and angrily walked away. He had seen the face of the Lord in a young Dutch Christian, and he was ashamed. It's not easy for our young people to be witnesses these days. Yet they still take their punishment joyfully, believing above all else they must be his witnesses whatever the cost.

Yet this incident is a light and momentary trouble compared to other persecution going on around the world. If you were a Mexican living in a certain area of Mexico today and wanted to practice your faith, you could be evicted from your home for leaving your traditional religion. If you were an Algerian and wanted to walk nine miles in the rain to the nearest Bible study, you'd have to ignore the death threats that come through your door just before you set off! If you were a Sudanese living in southern Sudan, you could be starving along with all of your relatives and friends and might possibly be facing the prospect of crucifixion for believing in Jesus. And if you were a Saudi Arabian and someone reported you for having non-Muslim religious material in your home, you could be arrested and tortured. If you happened to be a Rwandan Christian and looked like a Tutse in one place or like a Hutu in another, you could be hacked to pieces in retribution for the genocide that occurred in that country.

"But I'm an American," you say, "and I'm grateful for it after all these horror stories you're telling me. You're just giving me lots of reasons for staying put." You might then don your coat and hat and head out for your church prayer meeting! But how can you wait on the God of this world in prayer without becoming heartsick about the world of this God? If we come to the point of realizing the grace of God in sending his only Son to die for us, how can we not see visions and dream dreams? What will we do about all the wild, crazy ideas that will pop into our mind of how to reach a lost world and love the Babylonians?

If you never step out in faith, take down your harp off the gift tree, and sing a gospel song to the lost, you'll never know real joy. Until you are convinced that "there is no other name under heaven given to men by which we must be saved" (Acts 4:12) and God has given us the order to preach that name to the whole world, you'll never be fulfilled. As we do the work of the Lord, gifted or ungifted, we will find our fulfillment and reason for being. It is my utter conviction that he died for *all*—not some—and that all must hear about it. That keeps me on risk's edge in evangelism, wimp though I am! And I have discovered that "when I'm a wimp—then am I strong!" Anyway, you might just find, as you are obedient and start sharing your faith, that you do indeed have gifts you were unaware of.

When We Step Out—God Performs Miracles

One way to get the gospel out is to help each other in this area. Wives can help husbands—and husbands, wives. Sunday school youth leaders can encourage pupils, and students can turn around and inspire teachers. We can all help each other! Starting with that sermon on Lazarus, my husband has been a great encourager to me. When we were working together to reach kids for Christ, my husband believed in the gifts and abilities he saw in me long before I discovered them for myself! What's more, Stuart counted it his responsibility to make sure I had space to breath and room to grow to develop them. Our convictions left us no alternative than to *try* and make a difference in our own home area—both of us, together.

Stuart, though, is a very secure man—and remember, a man of quality is never threatened by a woman of equality. My husband was not threatened in any sense by the gifts he started to observe in me, which could have caused competition in our situation but never did. It was Stuart who insisted that I exercise my gifts. I remember his seeing the gifts I have for evangelism, for what we call "raw" evangelism with youngsters on the streets of Europe. We asked for churches to open their doors to the hundreds of kids who had spilled out from their homes and were living in derelict houses and on the streets. But it was the fifties and sixties, and no church wanted to open its doors to that crew, and I suppose you couldn't blame them.

Then a man with a brewery offered us the use of his facility. He said, "You can use my brewery. We need to do something about these kids. We need to help them." So we said, "Thank you very much," and took it! We invited young Christians to paint murals all around the walls, like the catacombs. And then we went out on the streets and invited the gangs in. They were real tough youngsters. We called the transformed brewery the Bar-None, which was a mistake to begin with! (We learned our hard lessons as we went along.) We should have called it the Bar-Some because we learned we needed to keep some of the troublemakers out, but we didn't know that yet. So the first night we waited for thirty or forty kids to show up. We had a Christian band lined up for the opening night. It was the beginning of the Beatles era, and everybody in church seemed to have a guitar; everyone was singing Christian music, making it up as they went along. So we roped in some of these Christian kids and put them up in front of their peers. They were frightened out of their minds! We were frightened out of our minds, too. We didn't know how many of these wild young people would come into our coffeehouse.

On the first night one thousand plus came, packing out the brewery. The atmosphere was absolutely electric. We began to be baptized in what later was called coffee-bar evangelism. That's where it all began—outside of London in a town called Guilford, in the Bar-None, all those years ago.

He who doesn't make a mistake doesn't make anything!

We struggled on that week—making our mistakes, but making progress too. He who doesn't make a mistake doesn't make anything, they say! Stuart would get up on the platform and preach his heart out for five minutes—that's all the time they would listen. The band would play, and then we'd get among them and talk. An hour later, on the hour, Stuart would get back up on stage and do it all over again. This way he would get through a whole sermon by the time the evening was over. We were really getting into this and enjoying it.

I had made some great friends with the leaders of these gangs. There was this young man who really liked me, and one night he said to me, "I don't want to see your face messed up."

So I said, "I'm glad; I don't want to see it messed up either."

He went on, "Because I like you, I'm going to tell you something. There's a gang coming in tonight that doesn't like us, see? They don't like you either, and they're going to get the platform party, so tell that husband of yours that that's what's going to happen. I'm just giving him a hint!"

So, not being able to locate my husband, I dashed out and found a policeman and begged him to come in that night. He looked at me and said, "You must be crazy! Think I'd go in a place like that with that mob? Forget it!" and off he went. So next I found my husband, and I told him, "We're going to have trouble tonight. There's a gang coming in." I was especially concerned because Stuart had asked me to give my testimony that evening, so I was sure that when I gave him this inside information, he, my protector and my head, would say, "That's fine, Jill, I'll take charge of this, and you just go backstage and pray."

So I said to him, "I'm sure you don't want me to give my testimony tonight now that you know this."

"Why not?" he replied.

I was totally taken aback. It seemed obvious enough to me—why not! "Well, the gang's coming in, and they're going to get us. My friend told me he doesn't want my face messed up (nor do I)—and I'm sure you don't want my face messed up either."

Stuart cheerfully interrupted me, "Oh, when they see a woman up there, they won't touch you. The Salvation Army often sends the women in first, and they seldom touch them."

I said, "I'm not the Salvation Army! Stuart, you're supposed to be protecting me—you're supposed to be my head. And I'm supposed to be this submissive little mouse. So I'll just go backstage and pray for you!"

He said, "Jill, I think you've got a story to tell, and I think you can tell it, and I think you have a gift, and I think you should use it." And he added, "I'll get up there with you. I'll be right there. Let's do it, Jill. These kids haven't rejected Jesus; they just haven't had a chance to receive him, so let's tell 'em."

So there I was! And sure enough the gang came in. I can see them now. They surrounded the platform, and the ugliest and most frightening one, who was the leader, stood right in my face. I took the microphone, and I was so scared it was shaking. Stuart had his arm around my shoulders, and he was urging me to "go for it . . . go for it." I was just aquiver, and suddenly the young man put his hand on my shoulder, and I panicked, looked up to heaven, and said into the microphone, "I'm coming, Lord!" which was extremely embarrassing because I wasn't! So when I didn't go, I looked around, and there he was—the gang leader, looking very startled! He started patting my shoulder, calming me down. "There, there, love; there, there," he said soothingly. Then he got up on the platform, and he put his arm around my shoulder, too, and said to the crowd, "Look what you're doing to this poor young woman. She's scared out of her wits!"

"These kids haven't rejected Jesus;
they just haven't had a chance to receive him,
so let's tell 'em."

I didn't like to tell him that he was the one scaring me out of my wits! So I just smiled and said, "Oh, thank you so much. Can you get them to listen to me for a minute?" And of course he rose to the occasion. He said, "Sure!" And then he glared at the crowd and said, "Don't you make one sound." And you can bet they didn't! So I said, "Thank you!" and I told them about Jesus and the love of God. Then the Cross, the Resurrection, and Pentecost. I was able to tell all those women, those lovely young women in the audience, many of whom had been abused and used—about the Lord. I can see them now, leather jackets, chains on their backs, hair dyed in all sorts of different colors. As I told them they were worth so much because God had taken so much trouble to make them and that Jesus had died for them, and they could know him for themselves, they listened closely. "You can open your heart, and Jesus will come in and forgive you no matter what you've done, where you've been, or who you are," I said. "Jesus Christ loves you to distraction."

I finished, at peace with God and with myself. God by his Spirit, his holy cleansing Spirit, could and would fill the lives of those who believed.

That night many, many came to the Lord, and suddenly in the middle of that talk a great shout of affirmation burst from my heart. A shout of "Yes, this is what I was made for! This is the Jill Briscoe I'm meant to be. Painted with the colors of my culture, gifted and trained and ready-made for this hour." Every day ordained for me had been written in his book and matched with my gifts and talents along with Stuart, my beloved counterpart, my parallel, my opposite. We, heirs together, were serving him. It was all joy—nothing like it in the whole wide world!

Gifts Follow Heart

My "talk" that night to that mob in the Bar-None left much to be desired where homiletics, structure, or cohesion were concerned! But I learned a huge lesson that evening. Whatever gift I was to discover came second after heart. Gifts should always come after heart! A heart for the world that's going to hell in a handbasket is where it all begins! This is what pushes us beyond our fears and phobias. Gifts may or may not be discovered and developed as we get on with preaching the whole gospel to the whole world, but heart can literally take you to the ends of the world for Jesus' sake and make you incredibly effective. The Babylonians, believe it or not, are looking for someone to love them first—not lecture them! Someone with heart. That's where our witness must begin.

As God breaks our heart for the unreached, we will find that love takes care of our wimpishness, love will take care of our lack of giftedness, and love will result in obedience. It is the gift of love that we must develop: love for God, love for our neighbor, love for the lost. A love that obeys implicitly—no questions asked. "If you love me, keep my commandments," said Jesus. Our love for God, leading us to instant obedience to him, will take us into effective ministry and surprise us with abilities that possibly were there all the time.

But Moses said, "O Lord, please send someone else to do it." In other words, "Here am I, send Aaron!"

Take Moses for example. God required Moses to give his message to the pharaoh. After Moses had spent forty years in the backside of the desert as a fugitive and an alien, the Lord appeared to him and told him he was concerned about his people suffering as slaves in Egypt. "I am sending you," he told Moses (Exod. 3:10). Can you imagine how Moses felt when he heard that piece of news? At once he began to make excuses. "What if they do not believe me or listen?" he asked God. "I have never been eloquent, neither in the past, nor since you have spoken to your servant. I am slow of speech and tongue" (Exod. 4:10). In other words, I am not gifted. "The Lord said to him, 'Who gave man his mouth? . . . Is it not I, the Lord? Now go; I will help you speak and will teach you what to say.' But Moses said, 'O Lord, please send someone else to do it'" (v. 13). In other words, "Here am I, send Aaron!" The Lord, frustrated with Moses, replied, "What about your brother, Aaron the Levite? I know he can speak well. . . . You shall speak to him and put words in his mouth; I will help both of you speak" (vv. 14-15).

So Moses and Aaron begin to relay God's messages to Pharaoh. At first, things didn't go at all the way Moses expected, seeing God had promised to be with them. Pharaoh, angry with Moses and Aaron, made the lot of the Israelites even more bitter than before. Moses, devastated by this reaction and rejected by the very people he had come to lead, bitterly remonstrated with God. "I told you this would happen," he complained, "since I speak with faltering lips." Or putting it another way: "since I'm no orator."

What Moses was about to learn was that God can gift you with a powerful message and give you spiritual eloquence that will eventually get through. He can enable you to speak with spiritual eloquence—even with faltering lips—and achieve his purposes.

It is the Holy Spirit who gives us the ability to choose the life-changing words to accomplish his plans. Jesus said that his followers should not worry about how to defend themselves when they would be hauled into court and before authorities for their faith, for the Holy Spirit would teach them at that time what they should say (Luke 12:12). He didn't say that they would do it with the exquisite eloquence of an Isaiah. How they did it was secondary to the fact *that* they did it. Gifts put into practice would yield results in the end. After all, he said, "My word . . . shall not return unto me void" (Isa. 55:11, KJV).

We Need to Dream

So after loving obedience, then what? We need to ask God for the gift of a dream. Once God has gifted us with the gift of conviction that we must share Christ and we marry that conviction to the gift of love, we have to respond in faith and obedience, by asking him for the gift of a dream.

Where are the gifted dreamers? Doers we have in abundance, but where are the visionaries—the ones who dare to ask God for a dream? Believe it or not, a dream will take you where mere talent and ability, knowledge and expertise will not. Let me tell you about a young man who dared to dream dreams. His name is George Verwer. George was a student at Moody Bible Institute in Chicago. He had conviction of heart and a love for God that had started him out on the road of full-time involvement in kingdom business. Then God gave him a dream. George discovered that dreams are for the asking. The dream he had was that God's Word could break through the darkness in the least evangelized nations on earth. These areas began to be known in the evangelical world as the "10/40 window."

George and his roommate at Moody sold the little they had, bought an old van, and filled it with Christian literature. They spent their holiday break in Mexico distributing everything they had taken with them. After school, with Britain as their base, George and a small group of like-minded radical Christians began to mobilize students. They bought old vans, fixed them up, packed them with Bibles and literature, and drove them to India!

One day George and some of the Operation Mobilization team

visited a church in Britain to lead the Sunday services. They were looking for Christians to join them in this grand adventure. An elder in the church invited eight of these hungry youngsters along with George to lunch. At the end of the meal, George invited this man to be on his board! "I had just accomplished financial security," his new friend explained. "I was doing well and told George I needed to think about it. As I waited on the Lord that night, I decided it was better that I went under than OM went under, so I mortgaged my house, put the money to use, and thirty years later am still standing by. What joy to be still dreaming the dream, having played a little part in seeing it come to reality!"

I listened in awe as I heard the reality of that dream described. Now there are two thousand missionaries, and they are praying for two thousand more before the year 2000! They dream about every person on earth hearing the gospel by the end of the century. Crazy? Maybe—but George Verwer's team and his students are running and not being weary, walking and not fainting, on fire for Christ. Three hundred and fifty million pieces of God's Word have been given out over the thirty years since the dream started to become reality. As the leaders of that mission look through the 10/40 window, their vision is that the 90 percent of Babylonians who live in that unreached part of the globe will have a chance to "hear a song of Zion" soon—very soon. How much "gift" does George Verwer have to preach the gospel? A considerable amount, as it turns out. But it was his *dream* that gave him a better idea—the idea to mobilize young people in their college breaks and maximize their gifts, and put to use the gifts of thousands of Christian writers in books and tracts.

How to Sing under the Gift Tree

Have you hung your harp in the gift tree? Are you unsure of your gifts and talents? Do you feel overwhelmed and small beside other, "more gifted" people? Have you used your giftedness or lack of it as an excuse to refrain from doing the things that God's people must do? Has fear stopped your serving? Or do you simply not know what your gifts are?

One of the things that stops most of us from volunteering to help is the perfectionist attitude many of us have: "If I can't do it well," most of us say, "I won't do it at all." When we first came to the U.S., I wanted to be the very best pastor's wife. However, I didn't know how the very best pastors' wives behaved. So I made an elementary mistake of asking a bunch of people at church, "What do you expect of me as your pastor's wife?" They were delighted to tell me, and I just about passed out. As far as I knew, I didn't have one of the gifts they were expecting. So I relayed this depressing news to Stuart, who simply said, "Well, if you can't do it well, do it badly!" I found a Scripture that day that told me to "do it heartily as to the Lord," so I figured anyone could do it heartily and badly, and I got on with it.

Two things happened. As I began to serve the church as their new pastor's wife and did it heartily, badly, and visibly, some people took pity on me and came to help (that's how the work in the church began to be accomplished). The other thing that happened was that I discovered I *could* do things I didn't know I could. In fact, I never would have found out I could if I hadn't been willing to do them badly—for no other reason than the jobs needed doing and no one was doing them. Don't wait to be asked—identify a need, and begin to address it. In the executing of the task, you'll not only get a necessary thing accomplished but you may find your niche.

Another thing that holds us back is the time or money crunch. Perhaps we need to reexamine our priorities and live according to the priorities God has determined for us.

Have you hung up your harp on the gift tree because you felt you couldn't hold a tune? Let me ask you this question: Are you so convinced Jesus is the only answer for a lost world that you would sing a song anyway—gifted or not? Do you love and obey God? Will you ask him for his heart for the world, and will you dare to ask him for a dream? If you do, watch out! Who knows where God will take you before he comes or calls. But if you step out, you will find, gifted or not, a great shout of affirmation welling up in your heart as you see your dreams turn into reality and Jesus' kingdom come.

Why not take some time and dream. Let me give you an acrostic that you could use if you want to, once you've finished dreaming:

- **D**are to do something for God you've never done before. Ask yourself (a) What is it? (b) What's the first step to making it happen?

- **R**ead about other cultures and pray for them. Ask God to show you if you can "give" or "go."

- **E**xplore short-term church missions or trips to needy areas—inner cities or places abroad.

- **A**sk your pastor to put you to work. Ask him, "What needs doing around here—give me a test."

- **M**ake a promise to God to fulfill at least one dream a year.

Dreams can come true with commitment, hard work, and sacrifice. Dreams don't just happen to happen—we have to do our part.

LEARNING TO SING AGAIN

SPENDING TIME TOGETHER
For couples, families, Bible study groups, Sunday school classes, or for family devotions

1. In what order do these things occur: power, love, conviction, dream, gift, and obedience. Is the order always the same? Share from your own experience.

2. Divide the group into pairs. One person will pretend to be an unbeliever. The other person should explain the gospel as if it is the very first time this unbeliever has heard the name of Jesus.

3. Discuss ways to reach your neighbors, your city, and your world.

4. Pray about all of the above!

SPENDING TIME ALONE
1. *Command* follows *conviction* of the truth of the gospel. Read Acts 1. Do you believe this is for you or just the twelve disciples?

2. If you believe it is for you, what tools does God promise to provide for you to do the job?

3. Think of something you could volunteer to do that would give you an opportunity to practice sharing your faith. Write it down.

- What will you do about it?

- When will you do it?

- Pray about it.

4. Go to a Christian bookstore or library and read stories of men and women of faith who—gifted or not—accomplished much for the kingdom of God. (Ask your retailer to direct you to the books.)

5. Pray for those who are spreading the gospel around the world.

CHAPTER TEN

THE GERIATRIC TREE

Even to your old age and gray hairs I am he,
I am he who will sustain you. I have made you and
I will carry you; I will sustain you and I will rescue you.

Isaiah 46:4

A friend of mine whose responsibility it is, among other things, to oversee a ministry to the elderly was opening yet one more excellent elderly care facility. After he made his welcoming speech to the new residents, he joined them in a time of refreshment and celebration. After sipping a cup of tea with a newcomer, he realized she was a little confused, and so he asked her, "Do you know who I am?" "No," she replied with a sweet, encouraging smile, "but if you ask at the desk they'll tell you!" Those of us approaching the autumn or winter of our life can appreciate the anxiety such a story provokes. There is certainly much to concern us by this particular river of Babylon! It's very easy to hang up our harp on the geriatric tree.

I often speak to senior citizens who feel valueless in the church because the "younger generation" doesn't seem to need them anymore. "They feel that their modern way is a better way to go," complained one lady. Another woman felt intimidated by the new confident church leadership. "Their biblical knowledge is so great, and some of them have taken all these Bible study courses," she said. But leadership is lacking if it cannot affirm age and treat it with respect, finding places in church structures to use the wisdom of the experience gleaned from its older members. Committees should reflect the unity and diversity of the church as a whole, mingling age, race, and gender for depth and balance. "The young women in charge nowadays want to sing these repetitive worship songs that go on and on and on—the tunes are hard to remember or sing without music, and the words seem to lack depth and theology," another older woman confided. "I don't mind singing them, but I get so hungry for a good old hymn!" Hymn hunger is common among the older generation in many churches today. For these and many other reasons older people feel their opinions don't matter and their service doesn't count. It was not so in Israel.

Israel's Senior Singers

I bet there were not a few harps by the river Chebar hanging in this geriatric tree. No joy here! Or is there? Israel's history is replete with stories of its "ancients" singing their finest melodies in old age. Miriam, Moses' sister, was no spring chicken when she leaped around in the sand dunes tapping a joyful melody on her tambourine! She was even older than Moses, who tuned his harp to sing God's praises at the grand old age of 120!

Old age gives you the chance to sound a warning note. Aging should enable us to more readily admit our mistakes and share with others those failures in our life. It also makes it more likely people will listen to us—and that others may benefit. "You deserted the Rock, who fathered you; you forgot the God who gave you birth," sang Moses (Deut. 32:18). But he had lived long enough to add another stanza. "The Lord will judge his people and have compassion on his servants when he sees their strength is gone" (v. 36). What joy to live long enough to experience "the rest of the story" and be able to say to the world, "Rejoice, O nations, with his people, for he will . . . make atonement for his land and people" (v. 43).

Israel's history is replete with stories of its "ancients" singing their finest melodies in old age.

At the end of his life, David, the king of Israel, calling himself "Israel's Singer of Songs," composed one of the most beautiful poems of joy in the Bible. Maybe he gave it to the temple minstrels to sing. He, too, sang of the faithfulness of God to himself and his family (2 Sam. 23:2-5). Though the captives by the waters of Babylon knew it not, Elizabeth would sing her testimony to a faithful God at the end of her long life, even though her voice must have been cracked and worn. Her spirit song about Jesus would have surely raised the roof in the temple court if there had been one (Luke 1:42-45). None of these people hung up their harps in the geriatric tree. In fact, for some of them, their finest work had only just begun!

How old is old? "You're as old as you feel," say some. Well, that's not encouraging, is it? Actually you're as old as you are, which according to Scripture turns out to be just the right age as far as God is concerned! "The right age for what?" you may ask. The right age to join the choir of the ancients and praise the Lord. Retire we might, but, spiritually, retirement is out of the question as far as God is concerned. Didn't Isaiah promise that people would "soar on wings like eagles; they will run and not grow weary, they will walk and not be faint" (Isa. 40:31)? I want to be found hobbling along into my "exodus" days, humming my favorite hymn and hoping the people around will recognize the tune!

So the thing about getting old is that the wisdom accumulated through life's experiences—the things we did wrong and the things we did right—can become a place of blessing for others.

Gathering the whole nation of Israel together, Moses sang a song about the history of his people, reminding them of God's care. It was a refreshing song about "a faithful God who does no wrong, upright and just is he" (Deut. 32:4). It was a faithful song about a faithful God that was life-giving. "Let my teaching fall like rain and my words descend like dew, like showers on new grass, like abundant rain on tender plants," sang Moses (v. 2).

The songs we sing in our old age can be mature songs—comforting songs, fresh songs—reminding those who listen that a lifetime of proving God faithful is something to sing about!

More Years, More Mercies

Many a time I have sung this song of the fresh mercies and faithfulness of God to the younger generation. The older you get, the more able you are to compose such melodies because the more mercies you can recall! Young people particularly are thirsting to hear such good news. In a world where few are faithful and all seems insecure, such music introduces a clear, piercing note of hope and confidence in a disintegrating world of clanging discord. After all, if we can look back to real-life experiences of the Lord's presence and help in difficult periods of our life, we can tell ourselves and others, "He was there for me then. Why should he leave me now?"

The problems come so often when the hard shocks of life knock the wind right out of us—and who can sing when they're winded? I heard a speaker talk about James Michener and what kept him writing. He quoted Michener as saying, "When I was five, a farmer living at the end of our lane hammered eight nails into the trunk of an aging, unproductive apple tree. That autumn a miracle happened. The tired old tree produced a bumper crop of juicy red apples. When I asked how this had happened, the farmer explained, 'Hammering the rusty nails gave it a shock to remind it that its job is to produce apples.' In the 1980s when I was nearly eighty, I had some nails hammered into my trunk—heart surgery, vertigo, a new left hip—and like a sensible tree, I resolved to resume bearing fruit. Being hammered by life jolts us into using our maturity and experience to make a significant difference."

I love the line "I resolved to resume bearing fruit"! Michener's nails are not my nails, and my nails are not your nails, but if we can all be sensible trees, those around will benefit by the fruit of our adversity!

The psalmist in Psalm 92:12-15 is found busily harping on his harp about the joys of old age—righteous old age. There is certainly nothing to sing about in unrighteous old age! He likens those found praising God in the courts of the temple at the end of their lives to palm trees flourishing, fruitful, and fresh:

> The righteous will flourish like a palm tree, they will grow like a cedar of Lebanon; planted in the house of the Lord, they will flourish in the courts of our God. They will still bear fruit in old age, they will stay fresh and green, proclaiming, "The Lord is upright; he is my Rock, and there is no wickedness in him."

My great desire like the psalmist is to still bear fruit despite old age—but, more than that, to still be bearing fruit *because* of old age! How will I do this? By proclaiming that the Lord is upright and that he is my Rock! I'll bear fruit by shouting it from the housetops and singing it to the Babylonians by my waters of Babylon.

In Isaiah 46:3-4 we read:

> Listen to me, O house of Jacob, all you who remain of the house of Israel, you whom I [God] have upheld since you were conceived, and have carried since your birth. Even to your old age and gray hairs I am he, I am he who will sustain you. I have made you and I will carry you; I will sustain you and I will rescue you.

I am finding myself testifying to this very thing as I enter the autumn of my life.

A Lifetime of Testimony

I have just had the great joy and privilege of speaking to thousands of women gathered in the Rose Bowl for an event for women. As I pen this chapter, flying on to Dallas, I am reviewing the messages I gave and realizing that I have been testifying to the faithfulness of God throughout my life. Even at this moment it would have been easy for me to hang up my harp on any number of trees, and yet it has been such a thrill to tell of his hand on my life and his love in my heart. It's all been so "fresh," too. As I shared my story and how I came to faith (hundreds of years ago—or so it seems), a song began to be sung in that huge auditorium. As I told the women about the rusty nails God has allowed to be hammered into this particular "old apple tree," a great murmuring of understanding and affirmation floated out over the green turf in my direction from other old apple trees in the stands!

It's been hard work these last days—hard but infinitely rewarding—and now I'm on my way to join my husband at the dedication of our youngest son's growing church in Dallas, Texas. (The apple doesn't fall far from the tree!) Stuart will be reminding the next generation of the faithfulness of God to sustain and inspire his people to build Christ's church, and I know he will be speaking to the faithfulness of God in his own life and ministry. What joy. Truly "they that wait upon the Lord shall renew their strength; . . . they shall run, and not be weary; and they shall walk, and not faint" (Isa. 40:31, KJV). I can truly testify to the lifting, empowering strength that God gives me as I travel this world for him.

Not long ago I returned from one of the most significant ministry trips of my life. I had written for seven hours straight. The stewardess came by and said, "I give you credit—you have worked the hardest on this entire flight!" Yet the pen had flown (though the back was sore), and the joy of my experience demanded urgently that I capture the moment while I remembered all the songs of all the other harpists I'd been privileged to hear. I told the young stewardess why it had been all joy to write for so long, and she cast a hungry, vulnerable look at me as if to say, *I wish I had something as worthwhile as that to write about.*

I thought about the 180 women leaders from twenty-six Eastern and Western European countries who had gathered in Budapest, Hungary, under the Evangelical Alliance's "Hope for Europe" banner. They had come to hear what God had been doing through women and their ministries in their respective countries and to try to find ways to increase their impact. The host committee—Hungarians already overloaded—cheerfully committed themselves to going beyond the call of duty by serving Jesus and us. One member of their team landed in the hospital the week before the event but checked herself out in order to come to the prayer meeting, then checked herself in again! *Do I take such a serious view of prayer?* I found myself wondering (quietly of course—after all, I was the guest speaker!).

Highlights for all of us were the instructive, inspiring, and sometimes depressing reports on the spiritual state of different regions. The heartbreaking struggles against unseen evil powers wreaking havoc with the bodies, souls, and spirits of people were countered by "God sightings." "God sightings," we were told, were interventions by God in the affairs of men—and in this case, women. Some dramatic, some quiet testimonies to the changing, keeping, and dynamic working of the resurrected Christ spilled out over us like a great refreshing avalanche. Joy was everywhere! "How could anyone doubt the presence and power of the living God after this?" we asked each other. We had a God sighting of our own when a tiny Moldovian woman (an older palm tree), her face alight with excitement, told us how her forebears had sold themselves into slavery in order to reach Caribbean slaves. (*There must have been an easier way,* I pondered.) This small woman with a great big extraordinary God living inside of her told us proudly that she was a part of a small evangelical minority among her people who were born from that incredible no-holds-barred Christian heritage and was "busy enjoying 'dying daily for Jesus' as the apostle Paul taught us to." (You would think to listen to her she had just put the apostle Paul on a bus for Athens!) It was all so relevant, evident, and prevalent! As far as she and her sisters were concerned, God *was* and that was all.

I listened to this woman's aged wisdom and thought of the same apostle's words from his own aging perspective: "Therefore we do not lose heart. Though outwardly we are wasting away, yet inwardly we are being renewed day by day. For our light and momentary troubles are achieving for us an eternal glory that far outweighs them all. So we fix our eyes not on what is seen, but on what is unseen. For what is seen is temporary, but what is unseen is eternal" (2 Cor. 4:16-18). There was no doubt in my mind that many of us at that particular conference were busy wasting away. But it was just as obvious to me that there were just as many who were being renewed day by day.

The Special Gifts of Senior Women

"We women in my country are after the order of Miriam, Deborah, Esther, and Tabitha," another beautifully articulate daughter of Eve confided (a middle-aged fruit tree) with a spiritual sureness and the sheer joy of living, born out of her love for the Lord. We listened to reports that confirmed my belief that women are naturally gifted to network, reach out to other women, and offer support whatever their differences, even when their male counterparts are not cooperating with each other across denominational, cultural, or ethnic lines. Women talked of mentoring and mothering, comforting and confronting, organizing and planning that surely the men must recognize and appreciate.

Leadership is lacking if it cannot affirm age and treat it with respect, finding places in church structures to use the wisdom of the experience gleaned from its older members.

This is not to say that the gatherings were free of tension and disagreements. There are strong, aggressive Christian women around all such gatherings, and some of them unfortunately belong to churches that have suspicions about all women's motives and intentions. However, I noted that strong, aggressive Christian women can be tempered with the Spirit's grace and learn how to have a gracious and submissive attitude—not because they are women, but because they are disciples of Jesus who happen to be women! And guess who was helping them? That's right. Old gnarled palm trees, whose wisdom was being highly respected. Not all the older ladies felt respected and appreciated, however; there are some in the church of Jesus Christ who put their old workhorses—especially the female horses—"out to pasture" and leave them there. Two women who were Danish Lutheran pastors, together with a woman in leadership from the German Baptist Union, listened with amazement and sympathy to their sisters who live, in some cases, just a few hundred miles away but whose gifts and talents are not wanted, appreciated, or even considered relevant or biblical! They are looked down upon for being old—and being women. Is it a matter of male chauvinism, ignorance, genuine theological differences, or just a misunderstanding of biblical old age? All of the above. Meanwhile, people outside church boundaries are lost and waiting for someone to tell them Jesus wants to find them, while we waste precious eternal moments debating the debate!

The Legacy of God's Aged Faithful

The highlights of our time together came when East blessed West with tales of trouble turned into triumph, as we listened to the ways God had made a way for the daughters of the King to tell their world of Jesus. A Romanian woman spoke gently and very movingly of her peace of heart and mind as she comforted her little girl through days of secret police interrogation. Life had been a crucible indeed for those standing for Christ under Communism. We listened hungrily. Here was a woman telling us how her family had "borne the yoke" in their youth and yet now were having an impact on their whole nation in their old age in a way they could never have imagined. (*Does it take such long, cruel nails to produce such a harvest?* I timidly asked the Lord.)

There were reports of angels delivering people in the crucible and sometimes out of it. Women testified to either miraculous deliverances or the endurance and patience to suffer for him. (The fiery chariot was still busy picking up passengers, I observed, even in these days.) Such God-honoring acts of witness were followed by conversions in these Western European countries.

We heard a story of a grandmother living under severe religious repression, who would take her granddaughter on her knee and kiss her little ear, whispering "God loves you." Then she would place her finger on her lips to show the little girl they must keep their secret lest they be arrested. Time passed, and the grandmother, who loved Jesus, died. Communism collapsed, and the girl, now grown into a beautiful young woman, came across a pastor in the town square who was taking advantage of the new freedoms to preach the gospel. Memories were stirred. The girl walked up to the pastor and said, "Can you tell me about the God who loves me? Do you know who he is and where I can find him?"

> *We heard a story of a grandmother, living under
> severe religious repression, who would take her
> granddaughter on her knee and kiss her little ear,
> whispering, "God loves you."*

Why was I so moved by this particular story? Was it because I, too, am a grandmother nine times? Here is a lady I want to meet in heaven and hear from her own lips how God helped her compose such songs of hope while living among such fierce Babylonians! Women like this, painted with the colors and history of their cultures, talked long with each other, lingering over the teatime baked goods that each delegate had baked and brought to the conference as a gift. Well into the night they shared their hearts as well as their cookies and rose early the next morning to pray together.

"This next generation of European women are in good hands," I recorded in my notebook, "but they need help to pass the baton!" Some are doing it well—as Titus exhorted them—the older women teaching the younger women.

I watched practical love in action from both young and old. The "blessing tables" were filled with love gifts from West to East. Soap, perfume, toys, and books were exchanged. But the women I observed were themselves walking "blessing tables." I watched a young woman literally peel off her jacket and sweater and hand them to an older sister, who had a daughter just her age and size. *It was a shame I brought my favorite blouse,* I thought and was immediately ashamed that I'd thought it! I was thoroughly ashamed of the time it took me to follow the example I'd just been given!

One Woman's Impact

On Saturday at the end of the conference thirty-two hundred women from all over Hungary gathered in the Sports Arena in downtown Budapest. This sort of meeting for Christian women was unprecedented, and the press, rightly intrigued, turned up to see it all for themselves. On each seat there lay a beautifully produced glossy magazine for Christian women, entitled *Lydia,* and many women of the one million who had heard about it or received it were there to meet and hear Elizabeth Mittelstaedt—its founder and author. Elizabeth, along with Alina Wieja, a dynamic, well-educated, and respected Polish woman leader making waves throughout Poland for the Lord, led the conference in its final meeting.

Elizabeth told the people her story. Her roots were in the East. God had spoken to her as a young girl through a woman Bible teacher. Elizabeth could hardly believe that God would use a woman, and that day she prayed, "Lord, if you should ever need another woman to serve you, call for me, and I will give my life for you." From difficult beginnings and against all odds, God called, and Elizabeth responded, "Here am I, send me." *Most of us resort, like Moses, to "Here am I, send Aaron,"* I wrote furiously on my program. Like everyone else, I was sitting on the platform riveted by a beautiful "God sighting." A failed dental procedure left Elizabeth in constant pain, and she contemplated jumping off a bridge into a river. However, she was not in the habit of taking orders from the devil, and so she soldiered on to birthing her vision and dream—a Christian magazine for women. Everyone except God and her wonderful husband, Ditmar, discouraged—even opposed—the idea. It would never work, they told her. But Elizabeth was a woman loved by God, and she knew there was a world of women "out there" who needed to know that. If they could only come to know the God she knew, she believed that good news would save them as it had saved her from despair and self-destruction. Out of brokenness and pain (she had literally come to us from the hospital on crutches, fighting, on top of everything, Lyme disease), she spoke her powerful words. It was brilliant, it was joy—it was him!

*Closing my eyes, I see their faces. There are those
lit up by Jesus and those with no light of life
lighting the windows of their despair and darkness.*

What spiritual "theater" it all was. Elizabeth's incredible, gentle grace chased us into God's arms. The music—ethnic, contemporary, classical, gospel, foot stomping, soul-searching, nerve jerking, tear triggering—readied us for listening with our heart as well as our mind. Our heartstrings were plucked as a top Hungarian violinist hushed the crowd, and a Gypsy sang in her unique style about the countrywide revival that is happening right now among the Gypsies in Finland. Then a top Swedish pop star, having given up career, fame, and cash, blew us away with her contemporary music and drama. Add to that a Polish woman's foot-tapping traditional offering and seven hearty trumpet-playing young male students (severely in the minority but indeed suffering it all cheerfully for Jesus' sake) rendering some wonderful hymns of the faith! We stood to hear the reading of the Scriptures, and I observed people worshiping in a variety of ways with their bodies as well as their minds and voices! It was beautiful, and I sensed God's great pleasure. We heard testimonies from prisons and palaces, and lastly it was this old tree's incredible privilege to preach the Word of God and apply its life-changing truths to all of our hearts, habits, homes, and hurts. "It is not you speaking, but the Holy Spirit who speaks through you," the Lord reminded me very early that day, hushing my fears to sleep as surely as he hushed the waves to sleep when he visited our troubled universe all those years ago. *It never gets any easier however many years you add to your days,* I thought! His Spirit, his Word, and his power did the work, and women of all ages and nationalities responded all over the huge auditorium to the call to follow Jesus anytime, anyplace, anywhere! There weren't enough hands and hearts and handkerchiefs to go around! A medical doctor told me that she had offered God her life for missions; a crowd of beautiful, flaxen-haired Hungarian women buried me with their gifts of hugs and kisses; a troubled refugee begged for assurance. She had found a "home" in God, and it took a lot of effort for her to leave that auditorium and return to face the music of another sort in Russia. This surely was holy ground. But then anyplace his feet and our feet are standing on together is holy ground. And who would stand anywhere else? Not I!

God Will Always Have Something for Us to Do!

As I finish writing about my experiences, I look around me in this flying arrow in the sky. There are women all around me. Some are sleeping. One is wrestling with a three-year-old and a baby who is objecting loudly to ten hours of confinement. The young mother looks uptight. Where are they coming from and where do they go, these daughters of Eve? Do they know how very much they are loved by God? Who will tell them? I decide I will begin to sort through the urgent invitations from Poland, Croatia, Romania, Russia, Finland, Germany, Belgium, Moldovia, and all the other places I can't pronounce. ("Don't worry, *I* can pronounce them," the Lord assures me.) Closing my eyes, I see their faces. There are those lit up by Jesus and those with no light of life lighting the windows of their despair and darkness.

"So what about it, Jill?" I hear God asking me. But I'm only a woman, and a woman over sixty years of age at that. I'm a little travel-worn and ragged round the edges, and my bark is peeling; I've lost not a few of my branches, and I get worn down now and then with pain of my own. "Be my Miriam—Elizabeth, Anna," Jesus suggests, ignoring my whining. "It's a choice, Jill, a choice to let my Spirit lift your spirit as you wait on me. When you are spent, let my Spirit help you to be spent again. 'I will pour out my Spirit on all people. Your sons and daughters will prophesy. . . . Even on my servants, both men and women, I will pour out my Spirit in those days, and they will prophesy,'" he reminds me (Acts 2:17-19).

"Well, I guess that's it then," I say. "I'll pour out—and you pour in!" I fished out a pen and got out the map in the pocket in front of the flight magazine. *Where's Moldovia, Lord?* I ask myself with a giggle. *I should have tried harder in my geography class.* I think of the older lady from this small Russian republic who had invited me to visit the country she was trying to reach, and I begin to compose a series of messages in my head. I'll ask my daughter to come with me to Poland, I decide; she and I will both minister—the old and the young together flying like an eagle! I think of other young women I could begin to mentor and pass on the baton to. *Why, I think I'll speak about Isaiah 40 and Psalm 137, Lord,* I think, getting excited. "That's a good idea," he agrees.

Here we come, Babylonians—watch out, Satan, my harp is in my hand, and this old tree's heartstrings are being plucked in fine fashion by the fingers of God! May he grant me many more years of such service and joy!

Are You under the Geriatric Tree?

Try to be honest. Has there come a point in your life when you retired spiritually? "I'm too old, too tired, too misunderstood," you are saying. Try to be honest and ask yourself, Am I flagging or flourishing? Am I an old tree that's still bearing fruit? And if there's no fruit, why not? Have I given up on the Spirit's ability to take me as I am and produce the crop he wants?

How to Sing under the Geriatric Tree

One of the ways we can learn to sing when we are old is to learn from older folk while we are young. My husband was greatly influenced by a man, an encourager well into his nineties, who gave Stuart helpful suggestions about his sermons. Now my husband, in his sixties, takes time to write lots of encouraging notes to young pastors and leaders, modeling after his mentor.

How can you sing even when your voice is old? By using your experiences, memories, and wisdom to benefit others. By taking the time that younger, busier believers don't have to meditate and pray and listen. By asking God—as you always have—to show you one or two people in your own circle of influence with whom you can share Christ in whatever ways present themselves. By demonstrating to all around you that being old doesn't have to mean being discouraged or useless or irritable. Think of the testimony to younger generations of an old tree that bears life's blows without losing hope—or losing joy! So many youngsters today are hopeless about their futures and about the world's future. They are so tempted on every hand to give up and give in to cynicism and selfishness that they desperately grab for everything they can get. They need to see people who have lived through many years and pains and still have a positive outlook on life.

The bottom line, however, when it comes to maintaining your joy in old age, is to spend much time with the Ancient of Days, who never ages—the risen Lord Jesus. He will play the heartstrings of your lyre even when you are old and infirm and sitting by your own particular river of Babylon. God will create in us his own brand of musical joy, lifting our life above the ordinary and helping us toward home!

LEARNING TO SING AGAIN

SPENDING TIME TOGETHER

For couples, families, Bible study groups, Sunday school classes, or for family devotions

1. Read Ecclesiastes 11 together. Discuss the pictures. What aspects of old age do they depict? What is the point of the passage? To whom is it addressed?

2. Read 2 Corinthians 4:9-11. What strikes you from this passage?

3. Make a list of all the means of renewal available to us today.

4. Pray together about all of the above.

SPENDING TIME ALONE

1. What are your goals for your old age? What are your fears?

2. Which of the Scriptures in this chapter meant something to you and why?

3. Read Psalm 92. Where is this particular tree planted? How is this tree described, and what does this mean? What do you think the fruit represents (see Gal. 5:22-23)?

4. How can you be preparing for your old age when you are young?

THE GRATEFUL TREE

Enter his gates with thanksgiving;
go into his courts with praise.
Give thanks to him and bless his name.
Psalm 100:4, NLT

In the end, joy dies when we do not practice it.

Joy is produced by praise glancing heavenward, feeling its soul begin to smile. Joy is Jesus—God in Galilean cloth, walking our earth, bearing our cross, burying our sin with him, and rising again to offer us life. For the joy that was set before him, Jesus endured the cross, despising the shame, and is seated on the Father's right hand in glory (Heb. 12:2). He is busy preparing a place for you and me and anyone who will thank and praise him for his salvation. There is such joy in realizing we're headed home—especially if our homes down here are hard and loveless places to be. Joy is first and foremost produced by praise.

Joy is produced by perseverance, too. We must deliberately joy in the journey, however dark the night or rough the road. That takes an act of the will—to reach out a hand to find him and grasp his heavenly help, to seek in the dark until we see a glimmer of light at the end of the tunnel. As we persevere, there is joy in finding our frantic spirit held in his arms.

Joy is presence—his precious presence. As we practice the

presence of God moment by moment and day by day, month by month and year by year, our life will find meaning and rest. It is hardest to practice his presence when the sun comes out and the spring flowers cover the earth. But our joy will fade like the flowers of the field if we do not.

I have a problem with my lower back (who doesn't!). Sometimes it's fine, and sometimes it's not, and occasionally it puts me in bed or in the hospital. I have found I need to look after my relationship with my back when it's well, not when it's in poor shape—and that's hard. Why sit properly, refuse to lift heavy stuff, and ask for help when I'm feeling just fine? Yet if I don't pamper it when it's good, it's only a matter of time till I'm in trouble again. Likewise, we must care for our relationship with God when things are good and not just when life is painful. This way, when trouble comes, we feel so good that we hardly notice the bad spell at all. It's as if we're held above it on a cushion of joy.

Joy is something only God can give, for joy is his heart!

Joy is produced by praise, perseverance, and practice, and it is sustained by God. He has placed his ever loving hand upon our life, guiding and keeping us, connecting and blessing us. Joy is something only God can give, for joy is his heart!

So are you ready to joy in God? Start by being grateful for who he is. Then think of all the things you are grateful for. I am grateful for life and health and a roof over my head. I am grateful for our children, who love the Lord, and our nine grandkids, who are learning to do the same. I am grateful we came to America thirty years ago, and I'm grateful for my roots and heritage in our beloved England. I'm grateful for my church and my Christian friends and the gifts God gave me to serve with. I'm grateful for the thousands and thousands of miles flown safely in the friendly skies and for God's forever family I've met around the world. And believe it or not, I'm even grateful for the dark times, too: for pain and hospital stays, suffering, and the death of loved ones. I'm trying to be grateful for problems that haven't yet been solved and perhaps never will be, and even for pain that doesn't quit, because these things make me more grateful than ever that I'm a believer, that I'm a forgiven child of God. The hard times make me so grateful for Jesus, my Companion, Helper, Friend, and Brother, my Savior, Lord, and King. He is the lifter up of my head and my heart and my highest hope. He is the light of my life and the joy of my soul! I have determined I will not hang up my harp on the ungrateful tree, for then I would be choosing death rather than life, chains rather than freedom, tears rather than laughter, despair rather than hope.

May God grace us with the grace to be continually, everlastingly grateful, for therein lies joy!